Bratsk Station and Other New Poems

YEVGENY YEVTUSHENKO was born in 1933 at Zima, in Siberia, and now lives in Moscow. His poetry has been collected in several volumes and translated into many languages; audiences in France, England, Italy and the United States (which he last toured in 1966) have responded to his impassioned poetry readings. He is married to Galina Semvyonova, who traveled with him to Siberia to gather material for *Bratsk Station*.

TINA TUPIKINA-GLAESSNER, who was born in Russia and lives in South Australia, has made a wide variety of translations from the Russian.

GEOFFREY DUTTON is well known in Australia as poet, writer, and editor; he is presently a director and co-founder of Sun Books. For a number of years he was senior lecturer in English Literature at the University of Adelaide.

IGOR MEZHAKOFF-KORIAKIN was born in Russia and completed the B.A. and M.A. degrees at the University of Melbourne. Since 1962 he has been on the staff of the Department of Russian Language and Literature at the University of Melbourne.

ROSH IRELAND is a graduate of Gonville and Caius College, Cambridge. He served in the British Embassy in Moscow in 1957–58 and since 1959 has been lecturer in Russian, specializing in Soviet literature, at Canberra University College and the Australian National University.

BRATSK STATION
AND OTHER NEW POEMS

by Yevgeny Yevtushenko

Translated by
Tina Tupikina-Glaessner
Geoffrey Dutton
Igor Mezhakoff-Koriakin

With an Introduction by
Rosh Ireland

ANCHOR BOOKS
DOUBLEDAY & COMPANY, INC.
GARDEN CITY, NEW YORK   1967

Author's Preface

Two philosophies are now struggling in the world: the philosophy of disbelief, of pessimism, and the philosophy of belief in an enlightened future for humanity. I have seen the living incarnation of this belief in many wonderful people whom I met at Bratsk. In the new Siberia of today, a country which in the past was a huge prison measuring thousands of square miles but which now becomes the source of light for our homeland, I saw the symbol of this faith. And is not the very name, so familiar to us, of the Hydroelectric Power Station, Bratsk, meaning "Brotherly," a symbol?

I worked about two years in suffering and happiness on this poem which I named "Bratskaya GES," "The Bratsk Power Station." Strictly speaking, perhaps this is not a poem but simply my meditations, joined together by the controversy between the two themes: the theme of disbelief expressed in the monologue of the Pyramid, and the theme of faith. To some readers the abundance of historical sequences in a poem with such a modern name may seem strange. But at Bratsk I thought not only of the heroic labors of the builders of the power station but of all the sons and daughters of Russia who have given their lives in the battle for the realization of the highest ideals of humanity.

The labor of the builders of the Bratsk Power Station is rightly called a great deed. But this achievement was prepared by the achievements of all our people during the many centuries of our history.

It is not by accident that I have made so many historical digressions, turning to the immortal names of Russian literature and the Revolution, and to the name of the man who is dearest to us, Vladimir Ilych Lenin. I wished to remind our contemporaries of their duty to keep sacred and to keep alive the tradition of the Revolution with all their labors, with all their lives.

This poem does not pretend to absolute historical verisimilitude and to epic all-embracing scope. It does not pretend to reflect exhaustively the greatness of achievement of the builders of the Bratsk Power Station. Some portrait-like chapters are, it must be understood, by no means a complete gallery of likenesses of the builders.

It may be asked why I turned just to these, by no means unclouded, destinies. But my choice was not accidental. Through arduous human fortunes I wanted to show the most convincing example of the unbreakable faith which is the main triumphant theme of the poem.

Yevgeny Yevtushenko

Contents

Introduction

BY ROSH IRELAND

> *Lord, let me be a poet,*
> *Let me not deceive people.*
> Y. YEVTUSHENKO

The last decade has seen in the Soviet Union a striking revival of poetry. Interest in the great poets of this century has quickened. Accomplished living poets, under constraint in Stalin's time, have once again found access to the reading public. A number of young poets have come forward to write poetry of a recognizably new kind, to create a vast and enthusiastic audience not only for themselves but for the great poets they claim as mentors, and to transform poetry into a vital medium of communication, a vehicle of expression through which not only their own thoughts and emotions, but also those of the great number of people who make up their audience, can be revealed and recognized to be held in common.

The death of Stalin, followed by his subsequent desanctification, left a generation to learn to think for itself in a society in which no one had been taught to doubt. It has been largely through poetry that the resultant shock has been discussed in terms free of cant; through poetry, a generation has tried to come to terms with life.

The leading figure in the movement urging poetry to the forefront has undoubtedly been Yevgeny Yevtushenko, now a man of thirty-three. His poetry and personality have caused him, within the space of a decade, to be alternately lionized and vilified by both East and West, treated as an unofficial ambassador of his country and accused of treason, compared with Mayakovsky and with Judas Iscariot, accepted as the spokesman of his generation and accused of cynical opportunism. The Soviet writer, whether or not under Stalin, indeed the Russian writer of any age, has had to bear a more direct responsibility for what he writes than writers in the English tradition.

Yevtushenko has not been alone. He himself has been quick to point out other poets whom time may show to have been greater than he, to play down his own achievement and constantly to intimate that he is unable to offer that which his generation needs. Yet among the group of young poets he has been the greatest versifier (technical competence being a feature of the new break-through), the one to take (in his colleague Vinokurov's words) "the mad risk of each new step," the widest-ranging, and of course the first public figure.

He is also of them all the most accessible. If one must pick one feature of Yevtushenko's verse to emphasize, it must be accessibility. His verse is meant to communicate, to find a common language with the reader, indeed to enlist the reader's sympathy, belief, and support—the obscure and the esoteric has no part in it.

Therefore, rightly, he has become the first and the best-known Soviet poet in the West.

His debut as a poet was inauspicious. He published in 1949 some anti-American verse in the newspaper *Soviet Sport* and became, as he puts it, "a real newspaper poet," supplying, in the Soviet tradition, occasional verses for anniversaries and holidays. Meanwhile he developed his poetic muscles by working with the technical devices of poetry —rhyme, meter, alliteration, and metaphor. His first book of verse appeared in 1952, but, he relates, left him with the sour conviction that it was the kind of book no one needed.

In order not to misunderstand totally the Yevtushenko who grew out of this "newspaper poet," it is wise to pay serious attention to what he says in his *Autobiography*, published by *L'Express* in Paris ten years later, about the death of Stalin in 1953, which he takes to be crucial in his life and in his poetry. He examines his own previous view of Stalin and reports on the literary situation at the time: the dearth of poets and the cynical careerism which controlled the Writers' Union, a characterization no doubt partly responsible for the viciousness of attacks on him by orthodox writers when the autobiography appeared. Then, in a passage now well-known, he describes the murderous chaos in the streets at the time of Stalin's lying-in-state and his answer to his mother "Yes, I saw Stalin," meaning that he had seen him in the stampeding crowd and the panic aggravated by the lack of orders from above. From this point onward, he sees himself combining and fusing in his work the intimate lyric, which found immediate response and the revival of which was one of the first signs of the "Thaw," and poetry with a social purpose, through which he hoped to indicate the wrongs of his time, yet, at the same time, to counteract nascent disillusion in his generation.

Yevtushenko's inability to answer for himself the questions he felt to be posed by the events of 1953 took him back in search of a reply to Zima, a small Siberian railway town two hundred miles northwest of Irkutsk, where he had been born and where he had spent the war years as an evacuee. The result was "Zima Junction," one of the outstanding poems published in the "Thaw" year 1956, in which he put his unanswered question to Zima, representing childhood, home, and roots. It is a long narrative poem, splendidly evocative of the small Siberian town, but full of episodes and meetings which indicate that appearances do not correspond to the underlying reality, whether the matter be marriage, youth, the authorities, beliefs, or personal qualities. All demand a re-examination, an affectionate re-examination but one which will reveal the faults and discrepancies of life.

Other poems published in 1956 in the collection *Enthusiasts' Highway* indicate where Yevtushenko is to find his answer.

Comrades,
> *we must give back to words*
>> *their original sound.*

Yevtushenko belongs to a family for whom the ultimate value is the Revolution. The importance of this cannot be stressed too much. He sees as the corrective for the confused situation of the fifties a return to the original values and ambitions of the Revolution, which represents for him not only an historical phenomenon, but a source of conviction and belief which he wishes to dissociate from the injustices of his time.

The years 1955–57 were triumphant ones for Yevtushenko, with books of verse published each year, but they were not untroubled. His marriage to the outstanding poetess Bella Akhmadulina broke up, the hardening of the official attitude to literature in 1957 brought him his share of rather pompous criticism, and exclusion for a time both from the Komsomol and the Literary Institute, where he had been studying. Following the pattern of an earlier difficult year, he returned in 1958 to Zima to write another long poem, "Where Are You From?" urging that no one should lose touch with his home ground, and declaring his faith in a generation that had demonstrated its solidarity and stood for truth.

By 1959, when a retrospective collection of his verse appeared, the "modern style" of Yevtushenko had become established and found its imitators. Its main features were striking and unusual rhyme schemes, based not on perfect rhymes but on assonance, alliteration, and association by meaning (any reader of Yevtushenko will find some extraordinary rhyme singing in his head for days); irregular meter—including extensive use of Mayakovsky's stepped line; and garish juxtapositions and bold metaphors (one thinks of the militiamen sticking up in their boxes like teaspoons in Russian glass holders). To these one could add a notable liking for antithesis: Yevtushenko, dealing as he does so often with discrepancies and contradictions, frequently makes use of antithesis in the closing lines of his poems.

The "fourth generation" of Soviet writers, those who had been too young to fight in the Second World War and who shared, as the critic Anninsky pointed out, a common background of evacuation and wartime hardship, had entered poetry and was soon to make its mark in prose.

With 1960 then began Yevtushenko's Wanderjahre. In quick succession he visited France, Africa, the United States, England, and Cuba. The span of his poetry widened to include occasional verse about his journeys, although much he published in his books of 1960 and 1962 does little beyond demonstrate his remarkable ability to turn verses on the small occurrences of everyday life. More importantly, he came forward as an interpreter of his generation abroad ("My Russia" in the London *Observer*, 27 May 1962).

To the same period belong the spectacularly successful "Poetry Days" and public poetry readings, which attracted huge audiences. These gave to Yevtushenko, himself a splendid, gripping reader of his own verse (he claims to have given 250 public readings in 1961), and to other poets the opportunity to try out their verse before publication (often long delayed), and assured Yevtushenko a community of emotions with his audience.

In 1961 he published "Babiy Yar," a poem on anti-Semitism. The poet's outspokenness on a topic of worldwide importance—a topic nonetheless most dangerous to broach inside the Soviet Union—brought him extremes of praise and condemnation and focused on him the interest of observers abroad. "Babiy Yar" was the first of a notable series of poems which includes "The Heirs of Stalin" and "Fears," the publication of which in 1962 was authorized within the context of an extension of Khrushchev's de-Stalinization (under the same dispensation, Solzhenitsyn's *A Day in the Life of Ivan Denisovich* was shortly to follow). The most convenient term to describe this series is "publicist," since in it Yevtushenko used verse as a vehicle for social and political commentary, for the poet's clear expression of his own views on the issues of his time. Yevtushenko attaches great importance to this public function of poetry—as in "Pushkin Pass," 1966:

> *Poetry is always the border guard*
> *at the frontier of the country's conscience.*

The year 1962 was a startling success for the younger

generation of Soviet writers. Yevtushenko's two new volumes of verse, *A Wave of the Hand* and *Tenderness,* came out in editions of one hundred thousand, and he himself was elected to the board of the Moscow branch of the Writers' Union and appointed to the editorial board of the literary magazine *Youth.* It seemed clear by late 1962 that the generation which had entered literature since Stalin's death, despite the disfavor with which they were regarded by a number of their elders, were being accepted into the official literary community under the aegis not only of officials of the Writers' Union and older writers who had encouraged them, but also of Party spokesmen. At the same time, the nature of their contribution to literature began to be seriously discussed. Taking part in this discussion, Yevtushenko was able, along with other new poets, to acknowledge his debt to Boris Pasternak.

Then came the first of a series of events in which Yevtushenko was to play a leading role, and which one must assume to have largely determined the nature of the poem which forms the greater part of this book—"The Bratsk Hydroelectric Station."

The details of Khrushchev's visit to the art exhibition in Moscow in November 1962 and the events which followed it are now well documented. It launched a campaign for the removal of abstractionist and modernist elements from the visual arts, a campaign which spread into a general move to restore socialist realist orthodoxy in all the arts, including literature. The new mood culminated in December and the following March in tense meetings between Khrushchev and his officials, on the one hand, and Soviet artists and writers, on the other.

Yevtushenko was drawn into the December exchanges both to defend abstract painters and sculptors and to clash over "Babiy Yar." Then, however, while official attention was shifting to literature, to Ilya Ehrenburg and Viktor Nekrasov in particular, he left to visit West Germany and France. In West Germany he spoke on international confidence and understanding, regretted the absence of diplo-

matic relations between the Federal Republic and the countries of Eastern Europe (except the Soviet Union), and sug-
gested the establishment of an independent Soviet-German
society to organize cultural exchange, all of which led to
his being taken for a semi-official spokesman for his country. In France, he published in *L'Express* his autobiography,* which reveals a man very different from the brash,
self-confident, doughty young literary lion of the Soviet
and Western press. It is full of the stories lying at the heart
of his poems, all episodes which are stages in understanding, revelations of the way of a world in which outward
appearance does not necessarily coincide with inner reality.
The autobiography is a development of his consciousness
of wrong—injustice, falsehood, and corruption (symbolized
by the eerie image of Beria's pale face in a car edging
along the pavement in search of a woman)—and a decision
to oppose it as a poet, to oppose it by presenting the ideals
of the generation of revolutionaries which perished under
Stalin to a generation which still suffers from the habits of
Stalin's time, and, in wider terms, to oppose the same faults
in both East and West on the basis of a belief in the essential goodness of people.

It is perhaps unfair to present the complicated development of a poetic consciousness in such bald terms. Yevtushenko may thereby appear to be a person of wild ambitions and woolly ideals. It is, however, essential to be aware
of the poet's view of himself, especially where the poet's
background is so alien to us, when coming to grips with a
poem like "Bratsk."

When Khrushchev spoke in March, he said that Yevtushenko had, on the whole, "behaved properly" abroad, and
warned him in only mild terms about his political immatu-
rity and aesthetic errors. Then, however, Yevtushenko became the chief target of violent attacks on the young writers made by conservatives at the Fourth Plenum of the

* The circumstances of the publication of the *Autobiography*
are examined in detail in Priscilla Johnson: *Khrushchev and
the Arts* (Cambridge, Massachusetts: Massachusetts Institute of
Technology, 1965).

Board of the Writers' Union of the U.S.S.R. and a similar
Plenum of the Board of the Writers' Union of the
R.S.F.S.R.* Of those attacked at the first of these meetings, only Voznesensky and Yevtushenko replied. The published report of his speech was indicative of what went
on:

"Y. Yevtushenko in the first part of his speech attempted
to 'dispute' the sharp criticism leveled at him. . . . However, under the influence of the exigent, principled atmos-
phere of the Plenum, Y. Yevtushenko was nevertheless
constrained to speak of his mistakes . . . (there follows a
long account by Yevtushenko of the distortion of his *Autobiography* by the French *L'Express*) . . .

"It must be said that Y. Yevtushenko's speech did not
satisfy those taking part in the Plenum: his speech clearly
contained notes which indicated that Y. Yevtushenko had
not recognized the roots of his errors, both in the case of
the publication of his *Autobiography* and in certain of his
verses."

Every aspect of his poetry and behavior, from his rhyme
schemes to his love poetry, from his misunderstanding of
Marxism to his flirtation with the "bourgeois enemy," was
condemned in most bitter terms, and he and the whole
pleiad of poets he had led were rejected and their sup-
porters and patrons jeered at. Yevtushenko was isolated
and, despite an obvious relaxation of the tension in the suc-
ceeding months and some guarded statements ventured in
his defense, his position was acutely dangerous. The poetry
readings and the foreign tours ceased and Yevtushenko's
career as a poet could have been ended.

It is possible to look back and minimize the results of
the Party's intervention between December 1962 and
March 1963. Yevtushenko's most virulent critics have ad-
mitted, at the Second Congress of Writers of the R.S.F.S.R.,

* R.S.F.S.R.—The Russian Soviet Federal Socialist Republic,
largest of the fifteen Union Republics which make up the Soviet
Union; it includes Moscow and Leningrad.

that they may have been unduly sharp in their criticism of processes which they considered wrong—in other words, that they far overstepped the mark in denouncing Yevtushenko and the others. The first authoritative statement in 1965 about the Party's attitude to the writers indicated a return to a position close to that of the end of 1962. It is evident, however, from his poetry that Party criticism had a profound effect upon Yevtushenko. And indeed it was only toward the end of 1965 that his first book of poetry to appear since that time was published. He was left to reconsider his position, and neither the poems he has published in various journals nor "Bratsk" provide more than partial evidence of the result of his re-thinking.

It could not have been unexpected that Yevtushenko should have sought first of all to re-establish contact with his audience. In the summer of 1963, he left Moscow to spend some time in the far north and then, as he had done before in similar circumstances, returned to Zima, where he wrote the first poem to appear since his return from France, "At Zima Junction Once More." The poem is built round three episodes, each related to a vital factor in rediscovering his role.

The poet returns to Zima, again downcast, covered, he says, by the dust of his foreign travels and by the dust of unpleasant rumors about him. He is urged to read his poetry by members of the Zima Komsomol, apparently unmindful of his disgrace, and he finds himself accepted and encouraged as a "local" (zemlyak):

> *The hall understood. The hall was moved.*
> *And, gulping tears in my throat,*
> *I felt this as an advance*
> *against that which I had to do.*
> *And it seemed to me, little by little,*
> *that the walls moved apart,*
> *and there—in lights, in forest green—*
> *through the sirens of the Volga and the Urals*
> *the land called me approvingly . . .*

His rapport with his audience was established—and here one recalls Khrushchev's injunction to him to pay more attention to the opinion of workers. Then, in the image of a busy transport depot, he sees the land waiting for words from its "Plenipotentiaries," the prose writers and poets—thus re-establishing another article of his faith, that what he has to say is needed. Lastly, a woman standing by the local military commandant's office brings him to a resolution to defend his country

> *against wars, all hardships, any*
> *eyes glinting with ill-will,*
> *against the repetition of mistakes,*
> *against far too nimble careerists,*
> *and patriots on the surface only.*

Once he has satisfied himself that his audience is still willing to listen to him and that the country feels a need for the words of the poet, he states again his old belief in publicist verse aimed at both external enemies and internal dangers.

The majority of the poems he has published since 1963 have been about the North. Almost without exception, they are of high poetic density and of very high technical quality, reflecting the range of his poetic accomplishments from exercises in technical conceits to work with the traditional four-footed iambic. Much of his concern is, again, with his roots in the land, coming to terms with himself, and his role as poet. He himself, no doubt, is the drake which lands on the Pechora to draw sustenance from that river. Once again, he sees isolated episodes as the mirror of a general circumstance: in the failure of his shouts to wake a ferryman on the opposite bank of a river, he sees his inability to be heard in peasant huts; in a muddled conversation, he sees not only that people fail to understand each other, but also that they fail to understand themselves. In all these poems, his most striking metaphor of himself is as a communications launch in the far north, carrying mail and therefore conveying the thoughts and emotions of people, early in the season, when ice and wintry conditions made

it difficult for the launch to find a passage. When naviga-
tion starts, bigger vessels will appear and the communications launch, having done its job, will be forgotten. This
metaphor refers, of course, not only to the difficulties of
the "season" in Soviet literature, but also to a motive which
has recurred throughout his poetry: that Yevtushenko sees
himself merely as the pathfinder, the one to break through
in mistakes and compromises, ever unsure of his direction,
and to be followed by a greater figure.

If the predominant themes of his recent work have been
those already expressed in "At Zima Junction Once More"
—his own position in difficult circumstances, his roots, and
communication among people and with himself—he has
nonetheless been able to continue his series of publicist
poems. "Nefertiti," published early in 1964, suggests the
permanence of beauty, and therefore of art, set against
the transience of crude temporal power. The one hundred
fiftieth anniversary of the birth of Lermontov in the same
year gave him the opportunity to publish "A Ballad about
Benkendorf, Chief of Gendarmerie, and Lermontov's
Poem 'Death of a Poet,'" in which he equated a "divine
justice," which Lermontov had predicted for the officials
indirectly responsible for the death of Pushkin, with a
"poet's justice" awaiting all "phonies, gendarmes, and
suckers-up." Last year's "Ballad on Poaching," which, in
the form of a feuilleton in verse, exposed the chairman of
a Pechora fishing collective who depleted fish stocks by
using nets of too fine a mesh, could be taken as a parable
on too strict censure of young writers.

The power of these verses has been much subdued, if
one compares them with, for example, "The Heirs of
Stalin," but it is quite clear that Yevtushenko has encoun-
tered difficulty over this period in publishing his verse.

Yevtushenko published the first extracts from "Bratsk"
early in 1964. The whole poem appeared just over a year
later. It was written in years which were extremely difficult
for Yevtushenko, when, although the charges of disloyalty
which had been made against him were quickly dropped,

he was in official disfavor and was forced to find a new role for himself in greatly changed circumstances.

"Bratsk" is a long and discursive epic, the five thousand lines of which clearly represent a huge amount of work. It contains, as Yevtushenko explains in his introduction, his thoughts, assembled within the framework of a clash of two opposed themes. The themes are faith and its antithesis, lack of faith. They are further reduced to a contrast of free and slave labor, and they are represented by two symbols, the protagonists in the dispute. An Egyptian Pyramid presents the eternal futility of man's efforts to free himself; the Bratsk hydroelectric station appears as a monument to free labor achieved by the October Revolution and is, in an obvious extension of the symbol, the source of light for mankind. Within this framework there are a number of disparate elements which include invocations to Russia's great poets, a series of historical episodes, a re-creation of Bratsk itself, biographies of some of its builders, and an examination of the importance of poetry. The dialogue of the Pyramid and Bratsk is only an external unifying factor. One has to search for some internal unity.

"Bratsk" goes much deeper than any of the other post-1963 poems in the context of the poet's search for his relationship with his country and its people. He brings in his country's history, treating it as a number of episodes leading up to the October Revolution. He then tries to connect the Revolution, which he sees as the carrier of great ideals and ambitions ("We are not slaves"), with the legacy of Stalin, and in the connection to solve the problem of his own position as a poet anxious to be within the conscience of his people.

With the exception of a few aspects, duly noted by an official Party critic who gave a generally favorable opinion of the poem, Yevtushenko's history is not unorthodox. He is not sufficiently explicit (perhaps he cannot be so) in his reply to the challenge of the Old Bolshevik in the poem to be careful lest the light of Bratsk be turned against its creators. His reply, that one must be loyal to the ideals of

Lenin, is not explicit enough, at least for us, to accept his view of history as convincing support for his position. Perhaps he makes his most important political point in his insistence on finding the connection between the events of Stalin's time and the Soviet Union of the present day. Stalin's legacy is too often limited officially to past time.

There is Yevtushenko's usual unevenness in the poem: some brilliant sections, the success of which is largely due to his mastery of a variety of verse forms; a wide range of material; occasional unsuccessful lines and some disappointing sections, including one unbearably banal biography.

"Bratsk" is, however, a second autobiography. Besides Yevtushenko's view of history, it contains endless echoes of his earlier poems, from "Zima Junction" to "Babiy Yar," the coalescing of a coherent view of his errors in the past and a determination for the future, the repetition of many postulations from his original *Autobiography,* and a vast amount of evidence on his view of himself and his own generation.

One other aspect of the poem's inner unity should be mentioned. When he writes in his introduction that the characters appearing in the poem are examples of "faith," the poem takes on the aspect of a poet's search for people who share his faith, a need to find people who share his aspirations. Yevtushenko's poetry, inasmuch as it is the poetry of a leader, demands that others be in close support. Otherwise he is isolated, vulnerable, and disoriented.

"Bratsk" may leave the reader with the impression that in Yevtushenko the poet is servant to the publicist. This is not true of his work as a whole, as the selection of recent poems included in this book with "Bratsk" will make clear, for it reveals the striking range of response which Yevtushenko possesses.

"Bratsk" must be seen to represent some measure of compromise with the official balance of values and not a full expression of the poet's own ideas. To find the essential element in Yevtushenko's poetry one must go beyond the publicist verve, the technical brilliance, and the vividness of detail to a basic concern with the human condition. Then Yevtushenko comes forward, not as a revealing source of information about the society in which he lives, but as a poet whose value, like his inquiry, extends beyond the boundaries of the Soviet Union, and whose work is properly the concern of all to whom poetry is important.

August 1966

Translators' Note on Bratsk Station

To understand this poem of Yevtushenko's, it is essential to realize that the word "Bratsk," the name of the gigantic complex of inland sea and hydroelectric station and factories in Siberia, two thirds of the way from Moscow to Vladivostok, also refers to "brotherhood" in Russian, through the adjective "Bratskiy," "brotherly." It is obviously impossible to reproduce this in English with such grotesqueries as "The Brotherly Hydroelectric Station." Therefore, throughout this English translation, only the words "Bratsk Station" have been used. But the dual meanings of the name, as also of "light" meaning both "light" and "enlightenment," are basically and intricately linked throughout the whole poem.

Yevtushenko is one of the greatest poets of the modern age. He is important not only because of the intrinsic quality of his poetry, of such masterpieces as "Zima Junction," but for his unique stature as a poetic force in both East and West. A passionately patriotic Russian, he is also a highly sophisticated and much traveled man. Editions of his poems sell by hundreds of thousands in Russia, and millions listen to his readings; but he has also drawn vast crowds on his visits to the United States, England and Italy. He is not a member of the Communist Party, but a fervent believer in the ideals of Lenin, in what he calls throughout "Bratsk Station" the "Commune." Giving the word its original French impetus, he demonstrates its workings in Russian history and holds out the ideal of the future commune of mankind, the brotherhood of nations.

"Bratsk Station" gives, as no other work has done, the essence of modern Russia. It gives it all, the great writers and rebels and revolutionaries under the Tsars; Lenin; the Revolution; some of the evils of Stalinism; the corruption of some Stalinist bosses; the priggishness of some examples of modern Soviet man.

Siberia, the ground on which the whole poem lives, is

both the endless prison which engulfed intellectuals under the Tsars and political prisoners under Stalin, and today the source of light from Bratsk, built out of the virgin taigá, the Siberian forest, by people who now actually go to Siberia of their own free will, much to the astonishment of those who remember the prison camps.

In "Bratsk Station" Yevtushenko speaks in several voices: his own and those of the Bratsk Station and the Egyptian Pyramid, young and old Russians, the Angara River, a Jew. Some are idealistic, some cynical, some wise with suffering or age, some innocent. The flatness of tone and banality of thought in certain sections would seem to be quite deliberate, when seen in the context of the whole poem; it is a poem that must be read as a whole. Yevtushenko is a highly aware writer, and a master of organization. The enthusiasm and rhetoric of some of his idealistic poems may likewise seem naïve to us non-Communists, though God (or rather Lenin) only knows how the grinding pessimism and mincing ironies of some Western poetry must sound to the Russians. But Yevtushenko is desperately anxious to show that "affirming flame" which W. H. Auden begged for in 1939. It would be easier, or more natural perhaps, for a Russian to be a cynic or a nihilist, after the appalling destruction of a civil war and two world wars in thirty years. Even today it does not seem to be generally realized that in the Second World War alone twenty million Russians were killed, as against about half a million in the British Commonwealth, and three hundred thousand in the United States. In "Bratsk Station" the voices of the dead sound constantly behind those of the living.

It is extremely difficult to give any true impression in English of the range and quality of Yevtushenko's poetry. He uses every sort of idiom, from classical poetic diction to the colloquialisms of the different times about which he is writing. He uses a very wide variety of forms of versification, and his rhymes are so subtle that it is better not to risk trying to copy them in English, which in any case has different facilities for rhyme from Russian. Yevtushenko also writes in the style of popular songs, and parodies the

solemn efforts of amateur poets (which he admires nonetheless, for the genuine feeling behind them). There are
many ironical passages. He loves to play with the multiple
meaning of words, and indeed, as has been said, the whole
poem is based on a play on the words "Bratsk" and
"light."

Grateful thanks are due to Igor Mezhakoff-Koriakin and
Rosh Ireland for help in checking the translation.

Tina Tupikina-Glaessner
Geoffrey Dutton

BRATSK STATION

Prayer before the Poem

A poet in Russia is more than a poet.
There the fate of being born a poet
falls only on those stirred by the pride
                                    of belonging,
who have no comfort, and no peace.

There the poet is his century's image,
and the visionary symbol of the future.
Without shyness, the poet summing up
the total, all that has happened before him . . .

Can I do this? I am not a very cultured man . . .
My hoarded prophecies contain no promises . . .
But the spirit of Russia is soaring over me
and boldly challenges me at least to try.

And falling quietly to my knees,
prepared for death and victory,
I humbly ask for help, from you
great Russian poets . . .

Give me, Pushkin,[1] your harmony,
your speech, free and unchained,
your captivating fate—
as if in jest, to call down fire with words.

Give me, Lermontov,[2] your bitter gaze,
the venom of your contempt,
and of your soul secluded as a cell
where hidden in the silence of your harshness
breathes sister-like the lamp of human kindness.

Give me, Nekrasov,[3] while soothing my exuberance,
the agonies of your lashed muse—
at main entrances, at railways,

and in the open spaces of forests and fields,
Give me your inelegant strength.
Give me the old Assembly bell,[4]
so that I can go, hauling all of Russia
like the bargemen heaving on the towrope.

O give me, Blok,[5] your clouds of prophecy,
and your two slanting wings,
so that, hiding the eternal riddle,
music shall flow through all my body.

Give me, Pasternak,[6] your disoriented days,
the confusion of branches,
scents' fusion, shadows,
with the torment of this century,
so that the word like a garden murmuring
shall blossom and ripen,
so that, for centuries, your candle
shall burn in me. . . .

Yessenin,[7] give me for good luck your tenderness
to birch trees and meadows, to beasts and to people,
and to all others on the earth
that you and I love so defenselessly.

Give me, Mayakovsky,[8]
                    your boulder-lumpiness
                        your turbulence
                            your deep bass,
your grim refusal of appeasement for the scum,
so that even I
                    hacking my way through time
may tell of it
                    to comrade-descendants.

---

[1] Alexander Sergeievich Pushkin (1799–1837), poet and novelist. Several times exiled from the capital to his estate for his political views. Killed in a duel.

[2] Mikhail Yurevich Lermontov (1814–41), poet and novelist. Banished to the Caucasus for having written a revolutionary poem on the death of Pushkin. Killed in a duel.

[3] Nikolai Alexeievich Nekrasov (1821–77), poet. Son of a landowner, author of famous poems about the misery of the peasants.

[4] Assembly bell. The Vetsche bell, used to summon people to the ancient Assemblies of northern Russia, for the announcement of important news and for the making of majority decisions.

[5] Alexander Alexandrovich Blok (1880–1921). Leading Russian symbolist poet.

[6] Boris Leonidovich Pasternak (1890–1960), lyric poet and author of *Doctor Zhivago*.

[7] Sergey Yessenin (1895–1925), poet. After initial enthusiasm for the Revolution, he became disillusioned by industrialization. Briefly married to the dancer Isadora Duncan. He wrote a farewell poem in his own blood and then hanged himself.

[8] Vladimir Mayakovsky (1893–1930), lyrical and political poet. The greatest poet of the Revolution, he was also a revolutionary in technique and one of the leaders of Futurism. He committed suicide in 1930.

I Journeyed through Russia

I am past thirty. I fear the nights.
I hunch the sheet with my knees.
I bury my face in the pillow, shamefully weeping,
that I have squandered my life on little nothings
and in the morning will squander it again.

If only you had known, my critics,
whose goodness is so innocently under question,
how tender thundering condemnations seem
compared with my own scolding,
you would be relieved, if late at night
you found your conscience tormenting you unjustly.
When leafing through all my verse
I find this: by squandering myself so rashly
I have soiled the pages with so much rot . . .
but I could not burn it; it is scattered over the world.

My rivals, let us cast away flattery
and the deceptive honor of abuse.
Simply let us consider our own fate.
We have in all of us the one and very same
sickness of soul.
                    Superficiality, it is called,
Superficiality, you are worse than blindness.
You can see, but do not care to see.
Maybe it is due to ignorance?
Or maybe, from a fear to tear up by the roots
the trees beneath which we have grown,
not having planted even a fence post for the future!

And is not that the reason why we always hurry,
skimming the surface, perhaps getting down a few inches,
so that, forgetting courage, we frighten ourselves
with our task to dig down to the heart of things.

We hurry on . . . giving half answers,
carrying superficialities like hidden treasures,
and not from cold calculation—no, no!—
but from the instinct of self-preservation.
Then strength begins to fail,
and we can neither fight nor fly—
the pillows of phonies are already filled
with the feathers of our domestic wings . . .

I was tossed about . . . flung backwards, forwards,
by someone else's sobs or groans,
now into the inflated uselessness of odes,
now into the false usefulness of pamphlets.
All my life I have been elbowing someone out of the way,
and it was I, myself. Caught by blazing passion,
naïvely clattering, I fought with hairpins
where the call was for a sword.
My blaze was feloniously infantile.
I lacked full pitilessness,
and thus, full pity . . .

Like something halfway between wax and metal
I was ruining my youth.
Let everyone who enters on his life
                              make this promise now
to help those who ought to blossom,
and not forget to avenge
all those who ought to be avenged.
Let this avenging be not for the sake of vengeance,
but avenging, incarnated
in the name of righteousness and honor,
in the name of the establishment of goodness.
We won't avenge through fear of vengeance.

The possibility itself of vengeance does decrease,
and our instinct of self-preservation
does not safeguard but kill us.
Superficiality is a murderer, not a friend,
health faking sickness,

entangling in the nets of delusion . . .
By bartering our spirit for trivial things
we run away from the general issues.
The terrestrial globe loses power in a vacuum,
by leaving general issues till later on.
But maybe its unprotectedness
is just the alienation of human destinies
in this enlightened age, so accurate and so plain?

I journeyed through Russia, with Galia beside me,
somewhere towards the sea, hurrying in a Moskvich[1]
from all my sorrows . . .
                              The autumn of Russian vastness
around us was weary of being golden,
from rustling with leaves under the tires,
and my soul rested at the driver's wheel.
Breathing scents of steppes and birch and pine,
huge tracts of land were hurtling at me
at fifty miles an hour—with a whistle of wind
Russia was flowing past our Moskvich.
Russia wanted to say something,
and now, having understood some things better than
    anyone,
she thrust our Moskvich into her body
and sucked us in to her innermost being.

And, seemingly, with some kind of premeditation
hiding its essence till the last minute,
Russia prompted me suddenly, past Tula,
to turn in towards Yasnaya Polyana.[2]
And now we entered the faintly breathing homestead,
children of the atomic age . . .
hurrying in our nylon raincoats,
benumbed, we suddenly stood still, hearts failing.
Descendants of peasant envoys seeking truth,
we suddenly this very minute became aware
of all the same, the very same knapsacks on the shoulders,
of all the bareness of worn-out feet.
Obeying a silent command,

we entered a shady avenue
of leaves transparent with sunset,
named "Avenue of Peace."
And this sheer golden transparency,
not retreating from luckless human fate,
lifted vanity like leprosy
while not diminishing its pain.
And meanwhile—the master of this homestead,
invisible, kept us in his view,
and seemed to be present, everywhere around us:

                                            now gliding
like the gray-bearded cloud reflected in the lake,
then his long stride sounding
through the mist of a smoldering hollow,
then showing portions of his face on the coarse bark,
furrowed by cracks and wrinkles.
His brows were shooting upwards, shaggy
in the meadow among the tangled weeds,
and the roots exposed along the footpath
were like the veins on his great forehead.
And, not decaying, but regally aging,
crowning the enchantment with their sound, sound,
all around him rose the enduring trees
like his vast thoughts.
They strained to the clouds and the womb of the earth
roaring more and more fiercely,
and the roots of their tips grew from the sky,
into the depths where the tips of their roots stretched down.

Yes, up into the heights and down to the depths, together!
Yes, genius—tying the heights and the depths together!
But how many still live ephemeral lives,
in the shadow of great ideas, in vain . . .
Well, then, was it for nothing that the flame of genius
    burned,
for the sake of changing humanity?
Or perhaps the fact that ideas do not age
is evidence of their lack of power?

How many years have passed already, how many,
that our purity, as in a drunken state,
throws itself like Natasha Rostova[3]
into false experience—to a rake and liar?
Again and again, in reproach to Tolstoy—
do we forget, by hiding from the passions,
that Vronsky, in his soft-hearted cowardice,
was more callous than Karenin.
And Tolstoy himself, swayed by his own reasons,
isn't he an example of his own weakness,
raving helplessly, like Levin,
in the blissful effort of making changes?

The labor of geniuses at times frightens
themselves with doubtful results,
but for each of them, broader issues
are won as in battle—inch by inch.

The three greatest names of Russia,
let them guard us from our fears.
Through them Russia was born anew
and will be born anew again.

When speechless and unseeing
she tramped through lashes, cudgels,
came Pushkin, simple, translucent,
like her self-realization.

When she had tasted lack of justice,
seeking for her sorrows' source
like the understanding of a ripened awareness,
came Tolstoy, pityingly harsh,
but with his hands tucked into his belt.

But when the way out was not clear to her,
and anger had ripened irreversibly—
Lenin burst out of the whirlwind, like the end,
and, that he might save her, blew her up!

Such were my thoughts, confused and airy,
on leaving Yasnaya Polyana long ago
and speeding in the Moskvich through Russia
with my beloved sleeping quietly on my shoulder.

The night was thickening, only faintly
                 pink light was spreading
along the rim of the world . . .
                 Lights flew into our faces,
accordions were singing boisterously.
                         A rusty moon
was toppling drunkenly behind the fences.
Turning somewhere off the highway,
I stopped the car, laid back the seats,
and with Galia floated into dreams
beyond the delusions of the stars—cheek to cheek . . .

I dreamed of a world
                 without the sick and the fat,
without dollars, francs and pesetas,
where there are no frontiers, no deceit of governments,
rockets and stinking newspapers.
I dreamed of a world where everything is freshly created
as a wild cherry tree stippled with dew,
full of nightingales and thrushes,
where all the nations are related and in brotherhood,
where no one slanders or abuses anyone,
where air is clean, like morning on the river,
where we live, forever immortal, with Galia,
dreaming this dream—cheek to cheek . . .

But, we did wake up . . .
                 our Moskvich stood daringly
on plowed land, its nose into the bushes.
I flung the chilled door wide
and beauty took my breath away.
Above the furious red, coarse, dawn,
a boy with teeth of steel drove a dump truck,
a cigarette pressed fiercely between his lips,

drove furiously, in the violent wind.
And furiously, like a blazing jet thrust,
over the darkness of the plowed land and the green of
    the meadows
the sun was pushing itself out
from a haystack's angry grip.
And the trees were fiercely denuded,
and the stream roared, leaping furiously,
and blueness was reddening and raging
swayed madly by the rooks.

I also would have liked to burst
as in fury, into life, unfolding a fury of wings . . .

The world was beautiful.
                              We had to fight
for it, so as to make it even better.

Once more I took a deep breath, settled down at the
    steering wheel,
and opened my insatiable eyes to:
Palaces of Culture.
                         Tearooms.
                                        Barracks.
District Committees.
                         Churches.
                                    Vehicle Inspection Stations.
Factories.
            Huts.
                    Slogans.
                               Little birch trees.
Jets cracking the sky.
                          Jolting of little carts.
Jammed broadcasts.
Overgrown statuettes
of milkmaids, pioneers, miners.
Old women's eyes, like those in icons.
Big-bottomed women.

Racketing.

Artificial limbs.

Oil rigs.

Slag heaps

like the breasts of a reclining giantess.

The men drove tractors.

Sawed.

Clocked in, then hurried to the tool bench.

They whizzed down into mines.

Drank beer,

Spreading salt along the rim.

Women cooked.

Laundered.

Mended, managing everything in a moment.

Painted.

Stood in queues.

Dug trenches.

Carried cement.

It was getting dark again.

The Moskvich was all covered with dew

and night was filled with stars to its declivity.

But Galia reached for our transistor,

and thrust its antenna through the window.

The antenna leaned against the universe.

In Galia's hands the transistor hissed.

Shamelessly, in front of the stars,

it boldly broadcast lies in many tongues!

O terrestrial globe, don't lie, don't play!

You have suffered enough, no more lies, no!

I gladly give away my posthumous paradise,

so that on earth there shall be a little less of hell!

The car was plunging into potholes.

(Road builders, what is the matter with you, silly bastards!)

It would have seemed that all around was chaos

but in it there were beginnings as well as ends.

There was—
           Russia.
The first love of the future.
And in her, undecaying through the centuries,
Pushkin somewhere began to bubble again,
Tolstoy grew more solid, Lenin took shape.
And, looking into the starry night, ahead,
I thought that great enlightenments
were joining together in that redeeming chain,
that maybe is only short of a link? . . .
Well, what of it, we are alive.
                          It's our turn.

[1] The Moskvich is a popular Soviet automobile.
[2] Yasnaya Polyana was the home of the novelist Lev Nikolayevich Tolstoy. It is now a national museum.
[3] Natasha Rostova is a character in *War and Peace;* Karenin,
Levin, and Vronsky appear in *Anna Karenina.*

Monologue of the Egyptian Pyramid

I am—
an Egyptian Pyramid.
I am wrapped around with legends.
And writers are guessing about me,
and museums are robbing me,
and scientists bustling with magnifying glasses,
timidly dusting, picking with pincers,
and the tourists
               sweating,
                       crowd around
to be caught in a snapshot on the background of
                              immortality.

Wherefore is the ancient saying
repeated by the fellahin and the birds,
that all people are frightened
                     of time
—but time is afraid of the pyramids?
People, repress the fear of centuries!
I shall be good,
             only I pray:
Take away,
         take away,
take away my memory!
In the harsh silence I absorb
all the explosive force of centuries.
Like a cosmic ship
                  roaring
I am taking off
             from the sands.
I am floating like a Martian mystery
over the earth
             over insect-people,
only some little tourist is dangling,
attached to me by his suspenders.

I can see through the nylon-neon:
countries are only outwardly new.
The world is all so frightfully old—
The same most ancient Egypt—
                              Alas!
the same meanness in her depravities.
The same jails—
              only modern.
The very same oppressions,
only more hypocritical.
The same thieves,
                grabbers,
                          scandalmongers,
shysters . . .
          As to changing them?
                              Rubbish!
Not for nothing are pyramids skeptical.
Pyramids—
        they are not so dumb.
Under me are New Yorks,
                      Parises . . .
Let me take myself in hand.
Let me lower myself closer
so I can gaze out over one country.
I shall move the clouds aside with my angles,
I shall cut like a vision through them.
Now then, sphinx by the name of Russia,
show your secret image!
I can see familiar sights once more—
only snowdrifts instead of sands.
There are peasants,
                and workers,
and clerks—
          far too many scribblers.
There are officials,
                  the army.
There is, probably, their own Pharaoh.
I can see some kind of banner . . .
                              scarlet.

But—
     I have known so many banners!
I can see
         new buildings piling up,
I can see mountains rearing up on their haunches.
I can see
        men toiling . . .
                   Rare sight—toiling!
In the past slaves were toiling . . .
I can hear—it sounds primeval—
their forests, the so-called taigá.[1]
I can see something . . .
              Not a pyramid?
"Hey, who are you?"
             "I am the Bratsk Station."
Yes, I have heard:
         You are the biggest in the world
you produce the most power
              etc. etc.
You must listen to me,
        the Pyramid.
I have something to tell you.
I am an Egyptian pyramid,
as to a sister
        I shall open my soul to you.
I am washed by the rain of sands,
but I am still not cleansed of blood.
I am immortal
        but I have no faith in my own thoughts,
and inside me there is nothing but screaming and sobbing.

Any immortality has my curse
if death
     is its foundation!
I remember,
        when slaves with moans,
straining under lashes and sticks,
were dragging a hundred-ton block
along the sand on runners made of palms.

The block was stuck . . .
                              the problem was to get it moving.
Without any hesitation they were ordered
to dig trenches for the runners
and lie down inside the trenches.
And the slaves lay obediently
under the runners:
                              as God had willed . . .
At once the block moved
                              along the slipperiness
of their squashed bodies.
The priest appeared . . .
                              with a dirty smirk on his face,
surveying the slaves' labors.
He pulled from his beard
a thin hair, smelling of ointment.
Personally he flogged them with a lash
and screamed: "Remake it, you lice!"
if the hair could be drawn swiftly
between the blocks of the pyramid.
And—
      swinging his fists,
bashing forehead or temple:
"You want to rest for an hour?
You want just a piece of bread?
Go and gorge yourselves on sand!
Drink bitch's milk!
Remember—not a hair!
Remember—not a hair!"

But the overseers gorged,
                              grew fat,
and whistled their song with whips.

---

[1] The taigá is the forest of Siberia.

The Song of the Overseers

We are the overseers
we are—
        your feet,
              throne.
On seeing us
        the Pharaoh
              sniffs
                  and frowns.

And what is he without us?
Without our eyes?
Without our throats?
Without our lashes?
The lash—
        is a medicine,
although it isn't exactly honey.
The foundation of the state
is direction,
           direction.
People without direction
would not be able to work.
The foundation of creation is direction,
                  direction.

The soldiers, gone soft,
would run like a mob.
The foundation of heroism—
direction,
        direction.
Those who are thoughtful are dangerous.
All thinking people—
              liquidate them.
Direction of souls
is more important
        than of bodies.

Are you making a din?
Are you whimpering again?
Wanting freedom?
But haven't you got it?
And voices, sounding not very cheerful,
    answer:
        "We have!
              We have!"—
Which might be that they have it,
or might be that they want it.
We are—
      the overseers.
We are humanely rough,
we beat you, but not quite to death,
and for your own good, fools!

With lashes
          cutting
into black
        backs,
to instill in them:
            "It is honorable toil,
the toil
      of the slave."
Why do you dream of freedom?
You have it, fools,
freedom—
         as far as it goes.
Your freedom consists
of freedom to be silent about your thoughts.
We are the overseers.
From us also runs
              sweat like a torrent.
Slaves,
     you can't blame us
            for anything.
We are vigilant.
We are dogs—
         only without muzzles.

But then even we
                    overseers—
are slaves to other overseers.
And over the groaning slaves,
Ammon's slave is he—
the overseer of all overseers,
our poor Pharaoh. . . .

The Pyramid Continues

But slaves aren't grateful for slavery.
Not mature, those slaves,
                              not mature.
They have no pity for overseers,
                              those slaves,
They have no pity for Pharaoh,
                              those slaves—
They haven't enough pity left for themselves.
And a groan went up along the ranks,

                              a groan of tiredness.

The Song of the Slaves

We are slaves . . . we are slaves . . . we are slaves . . .
Like the earth, our hands are coarse,
Our huts are our graves.
Our hunched backs are hard,
we are animals. We are bred for mowing,
thrashing, and yet for the erection
of pyramids—in order to exalt
the arrogant foreheads of Pharaohs.
You laugh at our fate, roistering,
in the midst of women, wine, boasting.
While you the slave is carrying posts
and the pyramids' rocky cubes.
Is it possible there's no more strength for the battle,
to rear up one day in revolt?
Surely it is not possible that in the eyes of poor people
this destiny is eternally repeated:
We are slaves . . . We are slaves?

The Pyramid Continues

And later the slaves arose,
paid the Pharaohs back for everything,
flinging them under the feet of the mob . . .
But does it make any sense?
I,
  Egyptian Pyramid,
tell you,
        the Bratsk Station,
how many slaves were slaughtered in riots,
but somehow I don't see any miracles.
They are saying
            that slavery is abolished.
I don't agree:
            it is even stronger,
the slavery of race prejudice,

slavery of money,

                slavery of possessions.

Yes,

    there are no old-fashioned chains,

but the people wear different chains—

chains of fraudulent politics,

                    of churches,

and the subtler paper chains of the news.

Here lives a little man,

a clerk, let's say . . .

He collects stamps.

He has his own little home on terms.

He has a wife and a daughter.

In bed he abuses the authorities,

all very well, but in the morning he brings reports,

bowing, nodding: "Yes" . . .

Is he free,

          Bratsk Station?

Poor fellow,

don't judge him too harshly.

                  He is his family's slave.

All right. But here

                in the presidential chair,

is a different sort of man,

and if,

       let us suppose,

                he's not even a rascal,

what good can he do?

As you know, apart from innovations

the chair is like the Pharaoh's throne—

                in slavery to its own feet.

Its feet are those who support,

and when necessary, restrain it.

It is tiresome for the president

that over *him*

              someone's "must" is hovering,

but it is too late to fight;

                fists are stuck

in flattery as if in dough.
Wearily the president sniffs:
                              "Oh, go to the devil!
I'm fed up with everything . . ."
Noble passions are dying out in him . . .
Who is he?
He is the slave of his own power.

You just think,
                Bratsk Station,
how many people are living
                            with oppression, fear.
People,
        where is your much-vaunted progress?
People, people,
                how confused you are!
I observe with my straight edges
and cracked sphinxes,
your many projects under construction,
your pigsnouting around,
                          and I see
                                    the spirit of man is weak.
It is impossible
                not to lose faith
                                  in man.
Man—
      by nature is a slave.
Man
    will never change.
No,
    I refuse flatly
to wait for something to turn up . . .
I am telling you
                 straight
                          openly
                                  Bratsk Station,
I, the Egyptian Pyramid.

Monologue of the Bratsk Station[1]

Pyramid,
        I am the daughter of Russia,
a country incomprehensible to you.
She was christened in childhood with a lash,
torn to pieces,
            scorched.
Her soul was trampled by the feet,
inflicting blow upon blow,
of Pechenegs,
          Varangians,
              Tatars,
and our own people—
              much more terrible than the Tatars.
And the ravens' feathers grew glossy,
but legends grew from the bones,
while fables of Russia's mighty endurance
built up throughout the world.
And then Russia's endurance became famous.
It grew to heroic stature.
She was kneaded like clay, with her own blood.
Yes, she did endure. That's all.
And to the barge-hauler, his shoulder rubbed through
                    by the straps,
and to the plowman, fallen in the steppes,
she whispered, with a mother's tenderness,
the eternal: "Have patience, my little son, have patience!" . . .
I can understand it all, how for many long years Russia
endured famine, and cold,
and the inhuman tortures of cruel wars,
and the burden of backbreaking toil,
and spongers, lying as far as they could go,
and every different kind of falsehood,
but what I can't understand is this: how did she bear
her own endurance?

There is a feeble, pitiable endurance.
In it there is a total crushing of the inmost being,
in it there is a slavish obedience, a torpor . . .
Russia's essence is not like that at all.
Her endurance is the courage of the prophet,
who is wisely patient.
She has endured it all . . .
                              But only up to a certain point,
like a mine.
          And then
                    came
                         the explosion!

The Pyramid Interrupts
                              I am against
any sort of explosion . . .
                    I have seen enough!
Stabbing,
          hacking,
                    but how much benefit from it all, if any?
Just blood spilt for nothing!

The Bratsk Station Continues
For nothing?
          I am recalling the past,
repeating to myself again
prophetic lines:
                    "Foundations laid on blood,
                                        stand firm."

And above the cranes
                    and the scaffolding,
Pyramid,
          with the scoop of the excavator
I am lifting the Moscow of taverns and boyars' houses
                         aiming through the midges at you.
Have a look:
          in the scoop
golden cupolas
          are sticking out

over its teeth.

What has happened there?

Why are the bells

tolling full pelt, so sullenly?

---

[1] The Bratsk project was launched in 1958. Construction work was begun in 1961 and is now (1966) about three quarters completed. In addition to the hydroelectric station, there are enormous lumber mills, pulp and cardboard mills, and other plants for wood by-products. One of the largest aluminum plants in the U.S.S.R. is under construction there.

The Execution of Stenka Razin[1]

In Moscow the white-walled capital
a thief runs with a poppy-seed loaf down the street.
He is not afraid of being lynched today.
There isn't time for loaves . . .
                    They are bringing Stenka Razin!

The Tsar is milking a little bottle of malmsey,
        before the Swedish mirror,
                        he squeezes a pimple,
and tries on an emerald seal ring—
and into the square . . .
                    They are bringing Stenka Razin!

                One after another they're following,
and following his mother as fat as a barrel,
a little boyar is rolling along,
gaily gnawing a bar of toffee with his baby teeth.
Today is a holiday!
                    They are bringing Stenka Razin!

The merchant shoves his way in,
                        flatulent with peas.
Two buffoons come rushing at a gallop.
Mincing rogues—cheats . . .
                    They are bringing Stenka Razin!

Old men, scabs all over them,
                        hardly alive,
thick cords round their necks,
mumbling something,
                    while doddering along . . .
                    They are bringing Stenka Razin!

And shameless girls also,
jumping up tipsy from their sleeping mats,
with cucumber smeared over their faces,
come trotting up—
                    with an itch in their thighs . . .
                        They are bringing Stenka Razin!

And with screams from the soldiers' wives
amid spitting from all sides
on a ramshackle cart
he
      comes sailing
                    in a white shirt.
He is silent,
            all covered with the spit of the mob
                        he does not wipe it away,
only grins wryly,
smiles at himself:
"Stenka, Stenka,
              you are like a branch
that has lost its leaves.
How you wanted to enter Moscow!
And here you are entering Moscow now . . .
Right then
          spit!
            Spit!
                  Spit! . . .
You're happy—this is a free show.
Good people
            you always spit
at those
        who wish you well.
I so much wished you well
on the shores of Persia,
and then again
              when flying
down the Volga on a boat!
What had I known?
                  Somebody's eyes,

a saber,
    a sail,
        and the saddle . . .
I wasn't much of a scholar . . .
Perhaps this was what let me down?
The official beat me deliberately across the teeth,
repeating,
        fervently:
"Decided to go against the people, did you?
I'll show you!"
I held my own, without lowering my eyes.
I spat my answer with my blood:
"Against the boyars—true.
Against the people—
        no!

I do not renounce myself,
I have chosen my own fate myself.
Before you,
      the people, I repent,
but not for what
        the official wanted.
My head is to blame.
I can see,
     sentencing myself:
I was halfway
      against things,
when I ought to have gone
        to the very end.
No,
  it is not in this I have sinned, my people,
        for hanging boyars from the towers.
I have sinned in my own eyes in this,
that I hanged too few of them.
I have sinned in this,
that in a world of evil
I was a good idiot.
I sinned in this,
      that being an enemy of serfdom

I was something of a serf myself.
I sinned in this,

               that I thought of doing battle
for a good Tsar.
There are no good Tsars,

                  fool . . .
Stenka,

        you are perishing for nothing!"

Bells boomed over Moscow.
They are leading Stenka

                to the place of execution.
In front of Stenka

          in the rising wind
the leather apron of the headsman is flapping,
and in his hands above the crowd

                 is a blue ax,

                     blue as the Volga.
And streaming, silvery,

             along the blade
boats fly,

     boats

         like seagulls in the morning.
Stenka,

      over the snouts,

              and washtubs

                 and ugly mugs
of the liquor sellers

            and the money changers,
like light through the fog,
Stenka

     saw

        faces,
distance and depth in their eyes,
and in those eyes,

             morosely independent,
as if in smaller, secret Volgas
the boats of Stenka's ax were flying.
It's worth bearing it all without a tear,

to be on the rack and wheel of execution,
if sooner or later
                    something grows in those *faces*,
                                        menacingly,
on the faces forming on the faceless ones . . .
And calmly
            (obviously he hadn't lived for nothing),
Stenka laid his head down on the block,
settling his chin in the chopped-out hollow,
and with that head gave the order:
                                "Strike! The ax!" . . .
The head started rolling,
                        burning in its blood,
and hoarsely the head spoke:
                            "Not for nothing!" . . .
And along the ax there were not chips any more
but little streams,
            streams . . .
Why, good folk, are you standing,
                        not celebrating?
Caps into sky—dance!
But the Red Square is frozen stiff,
the halberds are scarcely swaying.
Even the buffoons have fallen silent.
Amid the deadly silence
fleas jumped over
from peasants' jackets
                    onto women's coats.
The Square had understood something.
The Square took off their caps,
and three times, thrumming,
                        the bells
                            struck.

But heavy from its bloody forelock
the head was still rocking,
                        still alive.
From the blood-wet place of execution,
there,

where the poor were,
the head threw looks around

like anonymous letters . . .
Bustling,
the poor trembling priest ran up,
wanting to close Stenka's eyelids.
But straining,
frightful as a beast,
the pupils pushed away his hand.
On the Tsar's head,
chilled by those devilish eyes,
the crown[2] began to shiver,
and, savagely, not hiding anything of his triumph,
Stenka's head
burst out laughing
at the Tsar!

The Bratsk Station Continues

Pyramid,
are you wounded?
Do come to your senses—
all this was long ago,
and in the excavator's hoisted scoop
there is only a handful of Russian soil.
But resounding,
indestructible,
in the midst of the kingdom of the forest and the beasts,
repeated
by turbines,
Stenka's words echo
"Not for nothing."
Pyramid,
scanning the centuries,
I am telling you—
and I will pledge my light for it!—
All who perished in the past for the sake of truth
did not perish for nothing,
no!
Take a look—

on the vanes of my turbine,
bubbling,
        shimmering,
                        bursting,
reuniting,
        pushing one another,
disappearing and rising again,
amid the spray
                in the blue hum
flows vision
        after vision . . .
I can see in the foaming mighty music
of Angara[3]
        and the Sea of Bratsk—
                Spartacus,[4]
                        John Huss,[5]
                                Münzer[6]
and Marat,[7]
        and John Brown.[8]
Throwing the launches and boats about
the waves roll
        trailing
the speckled smile of Bolotnikov[9]
and the gypsy's jeer of Pugachev.[10]
Showing through the breakers were
the Decembrists'[11] shakos,
the hats of the *Potemkin*'s sailors,[12]
and sheepskin caps,
                kepis,
                        Red Army helmets . . .
I am running ahead of you . . .
                        wait.
Our conversation will not be simple.
I shall draw out all the soul of Russia.
I shall drill down into the centuries.
I shall snatch with my light
                        from the past
sea-girdled Petersburg.

---

[1] Stenka Razin. Stepan Timofeevich Razin was a Cossack leader and rebel. His place and date of birth are unknown. At one stage he was so powerful that he proclaimed a Cossack republic in Astrakhan. He attempted then to establish his rule throughout Russia, with declared aims of absolute equality and the abolition of the boyars (the ancient Russian aristocracy), officials, and dignitaries. He was defeated near Simbirsk by the forces of the Tsar Alexius, and in 1671 was captured and brought to Moscow, where, after stoically enduring monstrous cruelties, he was quartered alive.

[2] Crown. Actually the *monomakh*, a bejeweled fur cap worn only by the Tsar.

[3] The Angara River flows out of Lake Baikal through Bratsk. Its water is exceptionally pure.

[4] Spartacus (d. 71 B.C.), leader of the slave revolt at Capua.

[5] John Huss (c. 1373–1415), Bohemian reformer, burned at the stake.

[6] Thomas Münzer (1489–1525), leader of the Peasants' Revolt in Germany during the Reformation.

[7] Jean-Paul Marat (1743–93), French revolutionary, idol of the Paris working classes, murdered by Charlotte Corday.

[8] John Brown (1800–59), American abolitionist. After the battle at Harpers Ferry he was tried and hung by the Confederate forces.

[9] Ivan I. Bolotnikov (?–1608), leader of a peasants' war at the beginning of the seventeenth century.

[10] Emilian I. Pugachev (c. 1742–75), leader of largest antifeudal rising of peasants and Cossacks in the eighteenth century. Executed in Moscow.

[11] The Decembrists were the leaders, mostly officers of the Guards, of an abortive mutiny in St. Petersburg in 1825, the aim of which was a political revolution. Five of them were executed in the Senate Square.

[12] The battleship *Potemkin* of the Black Sea Fleet, on which in June 1905 a revolutionary rising took place.

Decembrists

Over the Petersburg houses,
over the inflamed minds
of the Tsar and the Tsar's enemies,
over the medley of whistles and curses,
of churches, brothels, lockups,
like a crier
the blizzard writhed like an hysterical woman.
The blizzard was tattered by hoofs,
everything under the sky was hidden under snow.
Over the white surge of the pavements
the moon was weary, wasting,
like a saucer in the fingers of a spiritualist
shivering in the jets of snow.

A young actress was praying,
falling at God's feet,
that she no longer be a serf.
In thanks for her art
she was flogged today by her master,
to the delight of the house servants.

Some kind of zealous campaigner,
giving soldiers orders in the darkness,
taught them to drill, until morning,
taught them to shout "Hurrah" one company after another,
having decided that the essence of a patriot
is the teaching of "Hurrah."

Bulgarin hurried into the house, out of the cold,
and at once began to write a new report
on various private persons, and on the press.
He was a real artist at compiling his reports,
having decided that the essence of a patriot
is to be like a ferret, and nose things out.

Those poor fellows, the censors, were poring
over a free-thinking paper,
sweating, their noses were sniffing,
noses snuffling for something,
having decided that the essence of a patriot
is to search like dogs searching in their coats.

But somewhere again, where rebellious speeches
blared among punch and candles,
teasing those present with a hint of freedom,
Pushkin came rushing in, snow covered, with his verses . .
Little devils of flame were dancing
in the eyes of his friends and in the punch bowl.

And Pushkin, raising his hand
which was trembling in anguish,
like the shiver of unseen trumpets
in an unforgettable descant,
read the lines: "Pluck up your courage and understand,
arise, you fallen slaves!"

They were still little boys,
smoke clouds whirling from their clay pipes,
twirling lightly in mazurkas.
And so they should have lived—among kisses,
among splashes of jingling harness,
and jets of snow, and cries of joy.

But the tempting ring of spurs
did not deaden the moans
in their dishonored country.
And angry boys were growing up,
narrowing their eyes like men
and in their sleep searching for a sword.

But they were accused of treason
and drenched with stinking mud
by a stupid pack of informers.
The naïveté of all Bulgarins!

No treason to their motherland
was hiding in those boys.

But in the senate sat foul treason,
well-nourished and arrogant,
delivering speech after speech,
granting favors to curs,
while the peasants were caressingly squeezed
so as to harness them more firmly.

Treason squeezed out decrees,
afraid of truth, as of leprosy,
afraid of those who were poor, and orphans,
afraid of those who were simply young.
And being afraid, it tied down the strings
of all dangerously celebrated lyres.

Oh, only they were blessed
who, like traitors to treason itself,
not turning back at all,
went on to the scaffold's planks,
having understood that the essence of a patriot
is to rise in the name of freedom!

Followers of Petrashevsky[1]

Drums,
       drums . . .
Petrashevsky's followers are being taken to the scaffold!
Hoods for hanging,
               hoods for hanging,
like shrouds
       to their heels.
The army line
       cold, infernal,
and They—
       standing shoulder to shoulder.
There is an evil smell of the Senate square,
on the Semenorvsky parade ground.
The same snow—
            lying in blinding sheets,
and blizzards with the very same whine.
In each real Russian there is
somewhere hidden a Decembrist.
Drums,
       drums . . .
left-right,
       left-right . . .
There will still be barricades,
but for the time being—
             only the scaffold.
But for the time being—
          alarmingly,
the light of Russia is being executed by darkness,
the hoods,
       the hoods
are being pulled over their eyes.
But one,
       wrapped up in the blizzard,
silent and aloof,

secretly sees all of Russia
through the futile hood.
Across Russia goes Rogozhin;[2] tattered, face distorted,
among visions and lights,
      crying, blustering.
Myshkin dashes across her,
and among her banks and granaries,
among her prisons and orphans,
Alyosha Karamazov[3]
roams like a peaceful monk.
Hangmen, undoubtedly
fear doesn't let you understand
that you—
   not those under sentence of death—
have hoods over your eyes.
You don't see anything of Russia
her nakedness,
    her bareness,
her pains,
   her strength,
her freedom,
    her beauty . . .

Horses are foaming!
     Horses are foaming!
At the gallop comes the Tsar's decree!
Sentence of death has been changed
for sentence of life . . .

But only one man
     pitifully—
in a fit of humiliation
tearing wildly at his coat,
cried out praise to the Tsar.
Clumsily he made haste,
tearing hooks and loops,
but the coat would not come off,
grown to his body, for ever.

Drums,
         drums . . .
Those whose will is not strong enough
are fated to be slaves, to be slaves,
fated to be slaves for ever!
Drums,
         drums
and men of high rank.
Oh, in old Russia,
                     what jolly puppet shows!

---

[1] Mikhail V. Petrashevsky (1821–66), leader of liberal movements in the nineteenth century, and of a progressive political circle in the 1840s.

[2] Rogozhin is a character in Dostoyevsky's *The Idiot*, of which Prince Myshkin is the hero.

[3] Alyosha is one of *The Brothers Karamazov*.

Chernyshevsky[1]

And when, set down from the cart,
Chernyshevsky rose above you, the crowd—
the spirit of Russia's honor,
Chernyshevsky at the pillory—
you looked depressed,
but from the scaffold the whole land
was visible to him, like a huge question
"What is to be done?"

And when the sword was broken over him,[2]
you, the crowd, in passive shame
were silent, as if a gag
had been thrust into your mouth.

And when the soldier, young and clumsy,
lowering his eyes,
fastened to that skinny chest
the placard STATE CRIMINAL,
why were you, subduing your murmurs,
unable to tear away the board?
It became a crime
to rise against crime.

But brightly with a feeling of doom
from across the crowd
somebody's frail hand
threw him a flower . . .

He saw somebody's plaits
and recognized the little hand
with the golden down on the skin
and the faded specks of ink.
And then her slender shoulders,
her poor cotton dress,

and her eyes, where the candles of the Decembrists
were burning.

How old was she—seventeen?
But she was shining,
the incandescence of the Senate square,
a blessed child of light.

And with happiness and pain
he thought: the day will come
when awkwardly,
that hand will throw not a flower,
but a bomb . . .

---

[1] Nikolai G. Chernyshevsky (1828–89), writer and revolutionary democrat. He spent twenty years in exile in Siberia.

[2] "the sword was broken"—i.e. a sword was broken over the head of a man condemned to the pillory by the executioner, symbolic of the fact that he would like to kill him, but was not allowed to.

Stepan Khalturin[1]

For the third night Khalturin doesn't sleep.
He is sick—gravely, it seems,
and under the pillow, breathing menace,
is his seditious dynamite.

A poisonous vapor
creeps, creeps up from the dynamite,
and his chest heaves with coughs again,
and his lungs are full of venom!

What will become of his dynamite?
Indeed, will it make him famous,
or else, will it poison others like him,
and never set anyone free?

Black-bearded, stooping, bony,
Khalturin wipes the sweat from his forehead—
half of him is Stenka Razin,
the other half is Decembrist.

His eyes are fixed somewhere in the distance,
and with his carpenter's hand
he strips off his soggy shirt
and lies down again, cheek to the sleeping blast.

Why, he himself doesn't know,
but suddenly it seems to him
that the dynamite is not dynamite at all,
but something timid, even peaceful.

The doubt grows in him and torments his soul.
Kropotkin,[2] Marx, Blanc,[3] and Plekhanov[4]
clash together in his soul, burning him,
and someone new who will come forward.

And this one shall be the avenger!
At this world of slaves and masters,
he, with eyes narrowing, shall brandish an idea,
and that will be—dynamite!

[1] Stepan N. Khalturin (1856–82), Russian revolutionary.
Executed in 1882.
[2] Pieter A. Kropotkin (1842–1921), anarchist leader and
theoretician.
[3] Louis Blanc (1811–82), French socialist.
[4] Georgy V. Plekhanov (1856–1918), Russian socialist and
Marxist philosopher.

Simbirsk Fair[1]

Fair!
    Simbirsk fair!
Better than Hamburg!
                  Hang on to your pocket!
Street organs are mumbling,
              and shawls are rustling,
and throats are shouting:
              "Buy here! Buy here!"
In the hands of the salesmen,
              telling tall stories,
there are light sables,
              and heavy brocades,
but the policeman is watching
              out of the corner of his eye
with his white glove
              on his little sword.
But at times he smiles
and his little white glove
jumps like a little fish
              up to his cap,
when in a light cab
              with a nice chick,
hiccuping, a king of caviar
              drives past.
And the king likes it,
              the way the kerchiefs part before him,
and the three-cornered hats
              and the caps,
and how a lady's lips,
              greased with pressed caviar,
glitter beneath her nose.
The bass voices of the market criers are roaring.

They trade in leather,
>   kid,
>   and satin,
kvas,[2]
>   holy pictures,
>   rotten meat,
>   and old popular romances.

And having sold her bag of spuds,
in the grip of the home brew,
a woman dances to a harmonica,
scarcely dragging her feet.
And she sings,
>   very provocatively,
getting tiddly,
holding her shawl by the edges as if she were still young:
"I have been to Oka,
eaten a-a-p-ple-s,
looking as if gilded,
preserved in tears.

I have tramped to the Kama River,
cooked my porridge in a pot.
The gruel was bitter with Kama.
Kama—river of tears.

I set out for Yaik,
got with my boy friend into a skiff.
Up and down along the stream,
sailing along a river of tears.

I went to the quiet Don,
I bought myself a home.
Isn't that a woman's comfort?
But tears came pouring through the roof . . ."

In her eyes everything is swaying,
her head is twisting.
She wants to be young again

and it doesn't come off.
And now the harmonica plays boisterously,
and now piercingly,

           like burdock burs . . .
Drink away, Russia,

           as long as you can,
only don't drink away your soul . . .

Fair!
    Simbirsk fair!
Be merry,

        everyone who wants to be merry!
But the woman is drunk

          and lies down in the mud.

And nice ladies,

        lowering eyelashes,
passing by,

      pass her by:

          "Simply horrid!

              Such a shame!"
a corn dealer

        passing by

          dodging by

            says from behind his beard:
"Look at her lying there . . .

          But who's to blame?

          Students!

            Yids! . . ."

And the philosopher—poor devil—
lowers his hat over his eyes,
and suffering proudly,

        passing by:
"There in the dirt, my people,

        you have found your fate!"

Is then life so base,

      just to lie and freeze in the mud?

But someone took her by the elbow
and quietly said to her: "Arise . . ."

Fair!
    Simbirsk fair!
In against the blue swings
                         there are shrieks
                                and whistles,
and the merchants' wives
                     hiss like geese in rage:
"A boy with a tart . . .
                  A student!"
He guides her carefully by the elbow,
he doesn't even realize that people are looking at him.
"Jesus bless you, honey,
                I'll be all right.
Somehow I'll make it on my own."

And he goes away,
                walking by the barges
on the Volga in springtime,
               and sadly she follows him with her eyes,
quietly blessing him
as if she were blessing her own child.
For a long time he wanders along . . .
All around it is getting dark . . .
The secret agents turn around
                  like squirrels in a cage.
But how could they sniff out
               who is the most dangerous
when in Russia all are suspect!
Poor agent. Listen, mate:
"The most dangerous one is always the one
who has to stop,
             who simply can't pass by
someone trampled down."
But the Volga is restless,
           snoring,
              moaning.

Birch trees over the river
                          light up the shadows
like timid candles
                    put up by the earth
for those who have suffered much on earth.

Fair!
      Russian fair!
Selling conscience
                    shame,
                            and people,
trading glass beads for precious stones,
and calling people in to buy
                              by every means.
You, Russia, they have squandered all of you,
and fooled you in the taverns,
but those who lied and fooled
will themselves stay fools!

Russia, you are tied and tangled,
but you were not born for slavery.
            Russia of Razin,
            Russia of Pushkin,
            Russia of Herzen,[3]
you shall not be trampled in the dirt!

They would have liked to see you drunk,
the Tsars,
          and the bureaucrats,
                                but you are strong,
and, even through moaning
                          as you fall,
you will rise again
                    all by yourself!

Fair!
      Russian fair!
The Russian paradise
                      brims with tears,

but a boy will come—
                    he will appear
                                again—
and with justice he will say
                        "Arise!"

The Bratsk Station Addresses the Pyramid

Pyramid,
            again and again
with foaming mouth I maintain:
the primary basis of revolution
is not anger
                but goodness.
When tears are pouring through the roof,
the system only seems to be indestructible;
revolution
is brewing,
and then the system
tumbles down.
Now I see proclamations,
coal flung at the villainous boss,
and inside me, not the roar of the waters,
but the furious cry of strikes.
And Russia is moving to liberation,
the blood of thousands reddening the earth,
from prisons, the shootings on the Lena,[4]
through the Ninth of January.
And in the fighting of 1905,
and in the May Days, with flags, waving,
and everywhere, shining clearly,
                                unstained,
that bright-eyed boy from Simbirsk.

Someone at nighttime,
                    covering his tracks, slips away,
someone hiding printer's type under his coat,
and, like lava from the throats of 1917
shatteringly:
            "Down with them!"

But again
          once more elbowing the truth aside,
lies are squeezing into power.
And now,
          Pyramid,
                have a look:
                      Petrograd. The Provisional Government.

And again a detective, suffering from flu,
hiding his nose in his overcoat
while even a great man[5] is forced, for the time being,
to hide his face under make-up.

What does he see in those faces shaking
in the autumnal pools? What does he hear
under the linden trees, hanging down like fishermen's gear?
What kind of thought enlightens him?

The October wind howls over him.
He is the embodiment of decision,
but he no longer can decide
and therein lies his greatness.

He enters someone's home, he looks
out through the window. Not a damn thing to be seen.
Russia drowns in damp darkness.
All around is solid dimness.

But light joins battle with the dark.
After a while, day will break,
and rain will tap with the secret knock
on the frozen glass . . .

The Pyramid looks on,
                    sees how heavily,
                              hugely,
snorting,
        the "Aurora" turns

as yelling thousands storm the Winter Palace.

The Pyramid looks on,
                              still skeptical:
"I see:
bayonets glimmering in the streaming rain
cold and implacable—
but justice, when it attains to power
becomes an injustice.
Such is the essence of the people . . .
One of the ancients made this pronouncement:
You can only understand a man
after he is dead.

There are no objections to this.
I agree, but not altogether.
You can only understand a man
after he has attained power."

But the Bratsk Station
                              its spray catching the light
roars through the flow of foam:
"But you must look once again at history.
I will answer you with Lenin!"

---

1 Simbirsk is a city about halfway between Moscow and the
Urals, and was the birthplace of Lenin, after whom it is now
named Ulyanovsk.

2 Kvas is a sour fermented drink made from rye or barley.

3 Alexander Ivanovitch Herzen (1812–70), Russian revolutionary writer. After being imprisoned for his political opinions,
he left Russia in 1847; he settled in London in 1851, and died
in Paris.

4 The Lena, a large river in Siberia, was the site in 1912 of
a mass strike of miners in the goldfields.

5 "A great man"—reference to Lenin.

Envoys Are Going to Lenin

Through country tracks
                    and villages,
with their sorrows
                    and their ailments,
envoys
        are going
                    to Lenin,
envoys
        are going
                    to Lenin.
Blizzards
        all around
                    are howling.
Hungry wolves are scouring.
But the peasants are seeking the truth,
for centuries
            seeking the truth.
So many of their generation,
who have seen all sorts of Pugachevs and Razins
were going,
            like them,
                        to Lenin,
But they didn't get there,
                        they didn't last out.
Envoys are going,
frozen, whispering the message they were given.
People
        stepping out for themselves,
people
        stepping out for all those who didn't make it.
But somewhere in Moscow
                        Lenin,
coming from Razin's Volga,
sees them on the telegraph ribbon

through all the summary reports.
He sees
          their faces are swollen.
He hears their raucous coughs.
He knows
          they are asking for footwear,
non-existent porridge.
The blizzard wails,
                    howling.
The frost warping
                the ranks of marchers,
and Lenin
          forgets about himself
but cannot forget them.
He knows
          that all ideas
are only empty "isms,"
if the tear-stained Russian huts
are in fact forgotten.

Horses gallop down the telegraph ribbon.
Children and women are crying.
                         The kulaks are hiding
                                          bread.
Typhus and cholera loom.
And bending to the howling wind,
stern and severe on the snow,
envoys are going like snowdrifts
                         to Lenin.
Going on
        marching
                across fields.
going on
        marching
                across fields,
Lenin—
      he is also Ulyanov,[1]
and they,
        they are also Lenin.

And through fires
                    constellations,
shots,
        shouts,
                    prayers,
invisible,
        Lenin is with them
going to Lenin.

But he can't sleep at night,
under his patched-up blanket.
Like a conspiracy
                    whirling in the ground wind,
the blizzard is prophesying to him:
                                    "They can't succeed,
your great ideals!"
In the sky,
        behind the clouds
the moon,
        like a waif,
hides
    from the Cheka.[2]
Devastation cries:
                    "It shall not be!
I shall swallow it all without trace.
It is not to be!"
                    The old whore falsehood
sniffles,
        "I am immortal!"
And sweaty faces
                    mockingly prophesy to him:
"That tart you lifted from the mud,
she will fall
            down in the mud again!"
"Into the mud with her!" hunger jeers.
"Into the mud with her!"
                            scream the speculators.
"Into the mud with her!"
                        laugh the counterrevolutionaries.

"Into the mud with her!"
whispers the hostile entente.

Every sort of nastiness
sticky,
mean,
cunning,

neighing,
squealing,
giggling:

"Into the mud!
Into the mud!"

The blizzard hatches a requiem,
but again, over Mother Volga,
he comes
simply,
Volodya,[3]
breathing the fresh air of freedom.
With inexpressible pain
the waves are rising,
spraying,
and in them
as in the soul of Russia
Stenka's boats are glittering.
The Volga is breathing resinously,
the Volga is drawling to him:
"Well, you student from Simbirsk,
is it difficult to be Lenin,
difficult?"
He can't sleep
he can't sleep
he can't,
but through the ruin and the blizzard
he sees living faces
like the face of an idea.
And for advice,
to the villages,
to their sorrows and sufferings,

Lenin
    goes
        as an envoy.
Lenin
    goes
        as an envoy . . .

"Yes," the Pyramid answered wearily,
"Yes, he is noble,
                yes, enlightened,
but looking at those people in vain does he have hopes.
I,
 for example,
            have stopped.
I pity Lenin,
            the idealist.
Cynicism
        is more comforting.
                        Cynicism won't let you down!"
But the Bratsk Station answers:
"Look around.
No,
    cynicism does let you down,
                        it breaks you.
By it all that is good in people
                        is crippled.
Cynicism—
        Cynicism is a latrine bucket.
Cynics—
        are the dead weight in the ship of mankind.
But idealists—
            are the helm and the sails.
I am not for the sweetly timid daydreamers,
childish in their complacency.
I am
    for those who are willing to fight
                    not for those who resort to prayer,
for idealists of action!

For those
         who have undertaken to change the world,
for those
         who are dragging mankind by the hair
out of lies and ignorance,
even if they don't act politely.
Mankind resists,
           it is dissatisfied,
not immediately understanding
that if it is hurt it is for a reason,
                    to save mankind . . ."
But the Pyramid gives its sharp-edged look:
            "Well, what of it—judge between us.
Where does salvation lie?
What if only the pain be left,
what if the salvation fails to come?
And what is the use of salvation,
               who wants it?—
freedom,
       equality,
             universal brotherhood?
Forgive me,
       I am forced to repeat myself,
but people—people are slaves.
             My friend, this is as true as ABC."
But the Bratsk Station rises against all slavery,
her waves are thundering,
              not surrendering:
"I know and remember a different ABC,
the alphabet of revolution!"

---

[1] Ulyanov was the original surname of Vladimir Ilyich Lenin (1870–1924).

[2] The Cheka was the secret police force operating in Russia from 1918 to 1925. The name is formed from the initials *che* and *ka* of two Russian words meaning "extraordinary commission." Its aims were "repression of counterrevolutionary activities and of speculation."

[3] Volodya is an affectionate version of Vladimir.

The Alphabet of Revolution

Aurora's echo[1]
> resounds
prophesying to the nations.

Elkina the schoolteacher
is at the front
> in 1919.
Oh, she should be reading Blok, Bryusov,
but she is holding a rifle.
Oh, she should have her fair hair done in plaits,
but they'd have been in her way when she aimed.
Now that the enemy has retreated,
there is a free hour,
and the Red Army men
> > are sitting on the grass like children.
Hungry, unshaven,
sick and wounded,
all good people,
all so illiterate.

Elkina the schoolteacher
opens the ABC,
slowly repeats,
repeats tenderly
drawing out
> each
> > syllable.
All right. But it's strange to these boys:
"Masha
> ate
> > her porridge.
Masha
> washed
> > her window."

They concentrate so hard—
but all to no avail,
those Stenka Razins
with their little red stars.

The schoolteacher, coughing,
stubbornly says it over and over again:
"Masha
         ate
              her porridge.
Masha
       washed
               her window."

But as if all this performance
had given him a rupture
                              the redhead
from Kostroma
bangs his rifle:
"Why you torment us?
What you teach us for?
Who is that Masha?
What sort of porridge?"

Elkina the teacher
almost bursts into tears
at this speech . . .
                          her shoulders
quiver a bit.
But the redhead
                  in distress,
talks to her pityingly
                          as to a little sister:
"Comrade Chalky,
don't cut up.
Big eyes,
          give us
sayings
to touch the heart—
then your lessons will get rolling . . ."

It was difficult to do,
but, breaking all the rules,
the very thing
    came floating out of her
like a call to battle
cutting into their minds:
"We are not slaves . . .
Slaves—we—are—not—"
And they repeated it
    absorbing it all,
and the one
   from Petersburg,
and the one
   from Eletz,
and the one
   from Baraba,
and the one
   from Kostroma:
"We are not slaves . . .
Slaves—we—are—not—"
Oh, such a clear morning!
How the steppe smells of flowers!
Why are you crawling along,
    schoolteacher,
with those useless bandages?

Oh, how ravishing are the daisies,
if only we could understand them,
    understand them!
Oh, how the birch trees are glimmering—
if only we could embrace them,
    embrace them!
Oh, how the streams are bubbling,
if only we could kneel down to them,
    kneel down!
Oh, how much I want,
want not to die!
But the horses are neighing,
    the roan and the mottled gray . . .

Soaring upwards, the bustards
brush with their wings
                         the sad,
empty stirrups.
All around are our young men
cut to pieces,
              all shot up . . .
And are you still searching for wounded,
teacher Elkina?
They are lying
               all killed,
among the flowering mint,
the one
        from Petrograd,
the one
        from Eletz,
and the one
            from Baraba . . .
But the one from Kostroma
still seems to be alive,
and only his eyes are strange.

"They shot me cleanly.
I'm ready to go.
Don't waste any bandages,
teacher, on me."

And, closing his eyes,
already almost gone
the redhead remembers something,
and he smiles, the redhead.
And already in the mist of death
painfully he breathes out the words:
"We are not slaves,
                    teacher,
Slaves—we—are—not . . ."

---

[1] The *Aurora*, cruiser of the Baltic Fleet, took an active part
in the October 1917 Revolution at Petrograd.

The Concrete of Socialism

"For centuries women were slaves . . ."
the kulak Zybnov was saying,
picking meat from his teeth
with a yellow nail.

And Sonka, a girl scarcely taller than a boot,
without father or mother
was wasting away in the kulak's house
like a sprig of wormwood.

Hiding herself in a corner,
overhearing rusty laughter:
"Well—now your Lenin is dead
the Commune will soon die too!"

Icon lamps flickered unsteadily.
Rats scampered in the passageway,
and the stripes on the Cossacks' trousers
were getting bloodier.

And the lash whose whistle is still
remembered in Petrograd and Baku,
is shoved somewhere into a flour bin,
waiting for quick reprisals.

Year after year was passing. Changing ice
to water, water to ice.
Sonka notched up her seventeenth year
in the roar of foul weather.

Blizzards were covering with snowdrifts
the regions near the Urals
but in the veins of laborers was singing
the blood stream of Pugachev.

And muffling her face in her shawl,
all in the snow, the whitest of white,
Sonka slipped out of the hamlet
and went on, and on . . .

In that drought-ridden steppe
that has neither edge nor end,
Dutov, the ataman of the Cossacks,
has executed her father.

And to the mountain, the magnetic mountain,
hardly able to walk any more,
Sonka went on, with only a prayer
that she find her father's grave.

But when she reached the Magnitka[1]
Sonka stopped, stock-still.
There was no grave, not even a trace,
but there were people, countless people.

And trucks were charging about like beasts,
and wheelbarrows thumping,
and frozen flags
were slapping with red ice.

And although the earth was like cast iron,
thousands of Sonkas were digging,
thousands of Sonkas were singing,
singing the song of the Commune.

And on all of them, digging and building,
lay a clean reflection
a certain good and simple face
unlike those you see in icons.

And one called Ilyich was looking sharply
at Sonka, narrowing his eyes,
thinking his own thoughts
as if expecting something from her.

And she took hold of a shovel
still warm from someone else's hands,
turned it around, clumsily,
and looked at her girl friends.

And gap-toothed Tamarka
said straight to her face:
"Hold your head higher, girl,
you are a Red navvy now!"

Sonka timidly jabbed at the ground,
as a farm hand once,
what else would she know but to dig,
a shovel handle is always the same.

And the first local mechanical excavator,
an imported job by the name of Marion,
faced up to Sonka's shovel,
completely subjugated.

Days flew from her shovel
like turned-up soil,
in the sultry heat and in the blizzard,
crumbling and clanking.

The grub of the Komsomol[2] members,
was made up of herring heads,
but—"Next stop the Commune!"
and, dig without saying any more!

Her quilted jacket is mended and remended,
worn and shiny, like a strap.
But keep your paws off,
you just try and touch our Sonka!

Sonka, so proud of herself
that she is not even embarrassed
by her torn boots
worn right through the winter.

And in the summer she proudly wore
two most terrible galoshes
from the "Red Triangle" factory,
tied up with string.

Only all alone and dreaming
she sees calf boots shining,
sailing somewhere in the distance
like miraculous ships.

A member of the Young Communists,
and of the International Workers Union,—
yet why are her eyes often wet?—
It is not like a Marxist to complain!

Petka, devilish concrete worker
in old Red Army hooded cap,[3]
couldn't you take some notice of her,
pay her a few attentions?

Well, Petka looks a bit startled,
"My problem is keeping up the concrete,
but my mixer has broken down again—
it looks as if it's a kulak sympathizer."

Putty is peeling off the windows
in the foreign specialists' cottages.
A dance is held near Mount Magnitka,
such a dance that the thump of it
could suddenly make the blue foxes
in far Alaska lift their muzzles to the sky.

The boys are dancing on the concrete.
Five forelocks flying, tipsy.
The boys are dancing
like mad country wine makers.

Their starred hooded caps
are leaping, dancing

the dance of the childhood of industry,
the dance of their own youth.

Never mind that this dance is heavy,
that feet get all clogged up,
never mind the building rattling,
if only the Commune will live!

Feet are moaning, feet are sinking,
but above the quagmire of the concrete,
The battle cry of Perekop,[4] "Come on!"
resounding, makes everyone shudder.

And in beads and earrings
forgetting Perekop for a while,
Sonka, the Red earth digger,
strolls around in her new calf boots.

For almost a year Sonka saved
her hard-earned rubles,
and, it's not clear where, she bought
those miracle ships, the boots.

In vain are you strolling, Sonka,
in vain are you thinking of stealing,
of stealing your Petka
from the dance.

Now then, Sonka, don't be prissy,
don't be afraid, come here.
That moisture on your lashes, Sonka,
is a bourgeois tear.

Your Petka's nose and forelock are dancing,
he plows along as in a blizzard
He is waving to you with his hand—
do forget about those boots!

And gay and lively,
so devilishly young,
the star on Petka's hooded cap
draws Sonka by its shine.

Sonka still cries a little,
but Petka draws her with his star,
and already with the tips of her boots
Sonka is probing the concrete.

Sonka scarcely sways forward,
her spirit is obviously weak,
and the boots have scarcely taken a step
before the concrete grabs them!

Sonka clutches to regain her balance,
her head is going round and round . . .
Sonka dances . . . but her boots,
her new boots are gone!

And flying like the cleanest spray
from her burning cheeks—what matter!—
onto socialism's concrete
fall the bourgeois tears.

Her boots are completely ruined.
It will be a long wait to get such things again.
Why are you darting about, unshaven,
dispossessed, Mr. Zybnov?

What are you nagging about, you scold,
gazing sideways over your shoulder?
"Dance, dance for a while—
you shall still reach the sticky end!"

Go away, don't cloud the light for us,
stay just as you are.
We shall dance to good fortune
even if our feet are raw with blood!

Sonka dances on, enraptured,
as if knowing in advance
that for centuries Lenin will not die
and neither will the Commune die . . .

---

[1] Magnitka is short for Magnitnaya Mountain, an outcrop of iron ore where the Magnitogorsk Metallurgical Works now stand.

[2] The Komsomol is the All-Union Leninist Communist Youth League. Founded in 1918, it now has several million members. Its community projects included the rebuilding of Stalingrad after the war. Bratsk is a Komsomol project; the average age at Bratsk is twenty-seven.

[3] The so-called "Budenny cap," worn in the Civil War.

[4] Perekop is on the northern end of the Crimean Peninsula, the scene of a battle during the Civil War.

Party Card

The heroic action advances
and everywhere Magnitkas are humming.
Communists are marching over the earth
like a million-faced Lenin.

Party cards in shabby overalls,
in women's jackets, in raincoats,
in much-laundered field shirts
and in mended jackets.

Party cards leading icebreakers,
going down the shaft with a song,
at Madrid, Khalkin-Gol,[1]
shielding the Commune with their bodies.

And the bullets are busily seeking
but there is no way out of it:
if the bullet is to reach the heart
it must go through the Party card.

Bullets only think that they are killing,
ceaselessly they fly, and still they fly,
but they are powerless to kill—they only
hammer the Party card into the heart.

Only he deserves a Party card
for whom, until the end of his days,
the Party card is a second heart,
indeed, the heart is a second Party card.

The Bratsk Station Continues

We shall be purer!—
Lenin is looking down from the banner.

It shall be purer!—
Magnitka roars immortally.
And from the distance a bass voice answers Magnitka:
"Here I am,
         your young brother—Kuzbas!"[2]
And following after, the strained hoarse voice of a steam
   engine:
    "Here I am,
             your young brother—the Turksib!"[3]
And from up there, where the stars are—a lively voice:
"I am 'Vostok One'[4]
           I am your youngest son!"
And rising up,
       across the waves,
I am Magnitka's daughter,
          the Bratsk Station!
Pyramid
    take a look:
        Over the space of time,
our banner beats and breathes and lives.
Pyramid,
    you have known many names,
       but one like this you have not known!
No,
  not all states are only outwardly new!
Revolution reared us.
Let it thunder over the world,
         as if to say: "I am against you!
Let us renounce the old world!"

For that reason, and that reason only, our banner
lights up like the dawn, with no false gleams,
so that never any more, anywhere on the earth,
shall there be Pharaohs, great or small.
For that reason, and that reason only, it flutters, roaring,
so that all nations be led to brotherhood,
so that justice,
      having come to power,
remain for ever justice.

It burns with vigilant, turbulent flame,
with the incorruptible flame of justice . . .
People, you shall answer with your conscience
for every thread in that banner!

---

[1] Khalkin-Gol is a river in Outer Mongolia flowing into
Lake Bhuir-Nhur. In May 1939 the Japanese invaded the Mongolian Republic and were defeated by a combined Soviet and
Mongolian army at Khalkin-Gol. As a result, the Japanese
agreed to restore the border and abandon their plans for north-
ward expansion.

[2] Kuzbas is a large coal and metallurgical center in Siberia.

[3] The Turksib is the Turkestan-Siberian Railway.

[4] Vostok One was the first manned Sputnik.

Reveille

Along the burnt-up steppes
across the hills and on the mounds
the weeds moan tonelessly
"I was killed at Rzhev . . ."

"I was killed near Rostov . . ."
The plantain rustles
through its sleep
under the dried-out, broken wheel.

"I was killed at Odessa . . ."
the gray stone repeats
like a sigh, shrouded in moss
and the spray of the sea.

Over our native land
the winds repeat
through each willow and mountain ash:
"I was killed . . . I was killed . . ."

And in the ashy soil, in the loamy soil,
there are so many fraternal graves,
wherever the snow settled,
wherever the rain poured down.

But all of you were laid
in spring and winter
in a common fraternal grave—
in our common earth.

You lie one alongside the other
pressing tightly together,
as in a trench in a storm
so it would be warmer.

And as together they have fallen
together they are lying—
the non-Party fellows
in one row with the commissars.

Because, in that battle
between two possible epochs,
all those who fell with honor
were commissars.

You did not part with the earth
but became the earth,
so that those who remained
could carry on your battle!

You fought near Moscow,
broke through near Kursk,
shielding the whole planet
from fascism with your bodies.

Shaggy-headed metalworker from Minsk,
Party leader from Donbas,
you saved Paris and New York
from slavery.

Wheat growers from Katun,
students from the Art Institute
with your deaths you saved
the possibility of the Commune.

There are rockets in our skies—
the hydroelectric station hums at Bratsk,
only the yellow broom whispers
"I was killed . . ." "I was killed . . ."

The flax bushes and the raspberries,
the daisies and the forests, whispering:
"Remember those fraternal graves,
remember, Bratsk Station."

Members of the Commune Will Never Be Slaves

The world was awakening
                              rustling, chattering,
when in the morning, along a dewy path,
we were led by the bandits to a precipice for execution,
at Kherson, in the region of the Volga, at Tripoli.
But we sang, and sang,
                              not bowing our heads,
tearing open our shirts across our chests:
"Never
        never
                never
Communards will never be slaves!"

We were gnawed and choked
                              by pitiless hunger,
we were swayed by the winds of typhus,
but we didn't fall—
                    made up of bones and sinews
and, also, of desperate faith.
Around us was poverty,
                    bare feet,
                                nakedness,
but we were building;
                    mining coal.
We didn't go begging . . .
                    Never,
                                never,
Communards will never be slaves!

Shatura was rising up,
                    Magnitka,
                                Kuzbas,
and bourgeois were scratching their heads . . .

So why then were we denounced
were we thrown
>   into camps
>   and jails?
But in you, Kolyma,[1]
>   and in you, Vorkuta,
we were wheezing, subduing our laments:
"Even here
>   we shall never
>   never
>   never
Communards shall never be slaves!"

And in the name of Russia and far-off Granada,
going in our vests against tanks with Krupps' label,
with the last bunch of grenades,
>   drawing on the last cigarette,
even though over many there is neither star nor cross,
but wormwood,
>   weeds,
>   wheat,
they are repeating:
>   "Never
>   never
Communards will never be slaves!"

We were tortured by SS men
>   burned with flame,
they persuaded us very kindly,
but we spat out blood at it all,
>   and we didn't join
their police or Vlasov's men.[2]
Leaving the blazing cities
we whispered with charred mouths:
"All the same, we shall win.
>   Never
>   never
Communards will never be slaves!"

And although we
                    did not know how to dodge and steal,
neither informers on the citizens
                                nor Beria[3]
got us to lose faith in Soviet rule,
to lose faith in the Commune.
And the Commune,
                not striking bargains with anyone,
we shall earn
            with our hands
                        and teeth.
Let it not die in us:
                "Never
                            never
Communards will never be slaves!"

.   .   .   .   .

Thus to eternity roared the Bratsk Station,
howling,
            throwing the waves into the attack,
while thinking it over,
            the phantom of the Egyptian Pyramid
                        disappeared in the dawning sky.

[1] Kolyma and Vorkuta were prison camps in Siberia during the Stalin regime.
[2] General Vlasov was a renegade Russian who fought with the Germans against the Soviet army.
[3] Lavrentiy Pavlovitch Beria, Commissar for Internal Affairs after 1938, was later disgraced and shot in 1953.

Ghosts in the Taigá

Those are not sweet-toothed bears
                              crunching cranberries,
those are not beavers whistling,
                              rising up on their hind legs,
those are not the screams of the brown owl
                              as if it were dying—
those are ghosts wandering
                              close to the Station at Bratsk.

Why do you look so sullen,
                              warden of the prison?
Is it that you have flogged too few men,
or with your ugly mug have you ruined
too few Tungus[1] women,
                              villain?
Now, at the Station, seeing a Siberian native,
you couldn't understand all this.
Your hand
          would twitch
                              for the lash,
but it has rotted away,
                              you old fiend!
Hey, you merchants,
                              why are you so wild with rage?
Why do you knock so angrily with your bones?
Why did you have to grow fatter all your life?
The result
is always the same—bones . . .

Gentleman gendarme,
                              gentleman gendarme,
how much you would have liked
to show your power to freethinkers
                              and other people like Yids,
but it is difficult to show it now!

Archpriest Abbakum, you are tired of irons,
the hair shirt of the fogs is cold.
What are you thinking of, by the Bratsk Station,
among the quiet,
                    childlike
                          Shamans.²

Hey, prospector, with your tireless pick,
the wood all moss-covered now,
have we found a precious vein,
or are we simply chiseling in the barren rock?

Oh, Petrograd's forerunners!
Lifting the same candles in your fingers,
tell your great-grandchildren:
from your spark flared up a flame
and is it the flame
you wanted to see?

"Clink—clank . . .
                    Clink—clank . . ."
                          The ring of the chains is sounding.
"Clink—clank . . .
                    Clink—clank . . ."
                                It's a long trek to Siberia.
"Clink—clank . . .
                    Clink—clank . . ."
                          Here, and there,
chains by the Bratsk Station,
                    are talking about us.
Give us your answers, chains:
                          Is it thus we should live?
Do we chew our black bread
                          rightly or wrongly?
Give your answer from the night,
partisans,
          librarians,
were you dying
              for us, such as we are,
or for others?

In the black forest
                I could hear
something breathing alongside me.
I felt a hand on my shoulder—
I shuddered:
                It was Radishchev![3]

"Long, long ago, over the place where the Bratsk Station
    is now,
I sailed on a frail boat,
with my teeth set on edge by guards and bitter berries,
but with faith in the lamps of my eyes.

When sunset dipped the world in dusk
and on the threshold of the sunrise, I thought
of the hidden strength of our people
hidden like the strength of these waters.

But looking into the wide, slumbering distance,
I didn't think that you could ever change
Siberia, Russia's ancient prison,
into the source of light of Russia's future.

Solemnly your mighty deeds
bear witness of your strength,
but let this strength still cherish in its depth
the sacred duty of compassion.

The supreme compassion is to struggle . . .
I can compose songs in an elegant style,
about seraphim, cheeks and breasts,
changing myself into a sated slave.
But someone's tears, some old nag's bones,
tormented my soul, torturing me
as my tired cart
rattled its way from Petersburg to Moscow.

Wanting to see my homeland changed,
I wrote from nature, without any anger,

but the body of the naked truth,

                    writing,
was crunched in the tender paws of the censor.

Those pinheads could not understand
that glimmering through these foggy pages
like the reflection of the dawn to come,
was a pure tormented love of my own country.

And it was banned . . .

                    A most imperial hand,
regally brief,
loving freedom without consistency,
imprinted firmly: 'Sedition.'

Then, a curly genius, freedom's fledgling,
accepting my crown of thorns
and longing for liberty and scope,
said:
        'Woe to the land where slaves alone
and flatterers may draw near the throne.'

But I felt the strength in this book of mine,
I knew it was fated to be saved,
to break through, to battle through, to shoot up.
I went into exile, pure in heart,
and wrote, as I remember, on the way:

'I am the same as I have always been, and shall be all
    my life—
not animal, not tree, not slave, but man.' "

Radishchev vanished . . .

                    I watched him go
by the Bratsk Station,

                    swallowed by the forest,

                              secretly
I thought of many things,

                    and it was not by chance

that I remembered
                    what the poet[4] wrote:
"salvoes of the *Aurora*,[5]
                    villagers uprising, palings in their hands . . .

But all this began at that moment
when Radishchev
                    with the sleeve of his uniform
wiped away a tear
                    on seeing an orphan . . ."

And I was thinking,
                    grown numb and quiet:
Are we worthy of such ghosts?
What sort of people are we?
                    Would each one of us
in his most difficult hour be able to say again:
"I am the same as I have always been, and shall be all
    my life—
not animal, not tree, not slave, but man."

---

[1] Tungus—native people of Siberia.
[2] Shaman—Siberian witch doctor.
[3] Alexander N. Radishchev (1749–1802), writer, revolutionary educator and materialist philosopher. Author of travel notes *A Journey from St. Petersburg to Moscow*.
[4] "the poet"—E. Vinokurov, a modern Russian poet.
[5] See p. 62, n. 1.

The First Wave

Ah, how silvery
are the rails of Urals steel!
O main line! Main line!

My Trans-Siberian line!
Tell me
      what is it
           you are yearning for,
amid the clatter and the flecks of light?
Or is it that you are glittering
from the tears that fell through the slits above you?
Do you remember
          how those eyes looked
out of the windows,
        renouncing everything?
How the shadows
      of iron bars
flew along the embankment?
And how, like pigeons
          breaking out
through those bars,
somebody's letters, folded in triangles,
          took to flight?
(Maybe someone will pick them up . . .)
They spun casually
over the pine trees
       and the mountain ash:
"Don't believe it
     my beloved . . ."
"Mamma,
    I am not guilty . . ."
There were many different lies,
many terrible things,

but don't,
        don't grieve,
my Trans-Siberian line!

The wind cuts across your path,
but obliquely,
           written with chalk
                  the sign on the carriage reads:
"The Bratsk Station is on the way."

Eyes talk to eyes
and to the taigá they have never seen before:
"We have 'banished' ourselves,
gone into astonishing exile!
Siberia, you must now become
                  the brightest of all lights!
Be joyful
        and give joy!
You who were once a punishment
                   turn yourself into
                     a reward!"

These young Moscow men and women
have organized an orchestral chorus,
and the Bratsk Station
rides along with red pigtails.

"I used to live on Sretenka Street
but now I have said goodbye.
I used to drink soda water
but the water of the Angara tastes better!
Mother's homemade rolls
were stuffed into my rucksack . . .
Taigá, my new mother,
please accept me in your family!"

Dear girl, you still don't know
how in that harsh first year
your fashionable skirt
will be torn up to wrap your legs,
that in your tiny tent

as it drops to forty-five below,
your red pigtails
will freeze to your folding bed.
Your poor feet will be covered with sores,
and a bear will scratch at your door,
and secretly you will cry
for your mother's homemade rolls.
Your hands will forget about manicure.
But you will survive, as all of them do,
in your mittens and your cap with its three flaps,
and your padded jacket and your tarpaulin boots.
And in this remote place
which once was an enormous jail,
you will build for yourself a Sretenka Street,
and a dance pavilion and a movie theater.
The Moscow people need not sneer . . .
you will have a manicure,
put on a bell-skirted dress
and stroll about in narrow shoes.
And in this dress you will
shine so you'll drive them out of their heads,
like a lamp whose light
you lit yourself!

All around the blue spruce
has tips of scarlet.
The Bratsk Station rides on
tossing its forelock!

Sing!
        Alyoshka Marchuk,
                        with your slightly Tatar look!
In conversation you are
                        so quiet,
you, but in song,
                so fierce.
May your seven-stringed guitar
play on into the morning

as if it were a seven-stringed
Angara playing!

(And do you know, Alyoshka,
with your cowboy's string tie on your chest,
that your life is still only the cover,
and the book of your future is to come,
that—Good luck to you!—
with your fine diploma
out there in the taigá,
you will thrust with saw and crowbar,
cram English by the campfire,
looking not at all heroic,
black as Satan,
with that cowboy's string tie
bind the sole to your boot in the mud.
And later, wearing the red band of the voluntary militia,[1]
you'll rush off at night to the place
where young thugs are fighting with knives.

And only in the morning, at dawn,
remembering with a smile your left hook,
will you find time to take out your drawing pen,
and it will fall from your hand.

But the hydroelectric station will rise up, and its light shine
    out,
and this song will start on its travels:
"Marchuk plays his guitar
and sings of the Bratsk Sea . . ."
And in distant New York City
your answers to students and the press
will be brief and awkward when you tell them about Bratsk.
Among the questions—some curly,
some vicious and penetrating—
someone will ask, suddenly,
                              like a schoolboy:
"How did it all begin?"

But no, it won't be the first tents
you'll remember, inwardly enlightened,
but those battered rolls,
and that train of singing people.

And, remembering all this, not without reason,
you will smile—so warmly—
and taking a beatnik's guitar
you will answer gaily:
                    "It all began with *this*.")

Hey, you bears,
                hide in the forest,
timidly,
        like sparrows!
The Bratsk Station is riding
with a guitar on a little string
Urals steel
            sing a song,
a song of strength,
                    and courage!
Railway of sadness,
                    become
the railway of joy!
So that on the rails
                    not a tear be left
of ancient sorrows,
and our souls,
                like rays of light
unite in one great light!
Into regions yet unknown
                        my country
surges
        on a wide sweep of foam
on the first wave.
Our lives
            are at stake
our sinews
            bursting.

It is harder for us
                than for anyone else,
the men of the first wave!
Who feels like us
                about the stars
and camp fires
              and the snow
and the sun,
we, the men of the first wave!
And this you must know,
                  my country,
that if it is hard for me
I am happy all the same.
                  I am
with the first wave . . . !

---

[1] Voluntary militia—Komsomol anti-hooligan patrols.

Red Flowers of the Taigá

"Where are you going, Granny?"
"On my way to the camp, dear boys . . ."
"And what are you carrying, Granny?"
"I'm carrying some red flowers, flowers of the taigá . . ."

In her hands, carelessly
bristling teasingly together,
red flowers of the taigá,
like little tongues of fire.
And looking sad and grand,
her swarthy face like one of Rublev's icons,[1]
framed under a spotted kerchief,
and her leather slippers
conversing with the earth,
she goes around the blueberries
so as not to crush them.

Birds and butterflies are flying
and the sun is burning,
and Granny suddenly
says quietly:
"I'd be walking along with my buckets
and, a couple of steps away, I'd see
those wretched, ragged people
in their rotting boots.
They were so thin and suffering from cold—
you just couldn't describe it!
And not at all like criminals—
with their clear, soulful eyes.

Ah, glory be to God,
freedom's been granted to them all,
and this mournful camp
stands quite deserted.

And today—I can't quite understand it all—
a whole train rolls in,
comes such a distance,
and all to build a dam.

For better or for worse,
these youngsters are here,
put for the time being
in the barracks of those old camps.

My elder granddaughters
were up at dawn,
and with buckets and rags in their hands
began to scrub the floors.

And my younger grandsons,
they even got up at night,
breaking up those dismal watchtowers,
tearing away the barbed wire.

Well, since morning people are simply
bringing things to the barracks,
some of them tablecloths, some, sheets,
some, cheesecakes, some, honey.

They are fixing up shutters,
laying down floor mats,
and here am I, old fool,
bringing red flowers, red flowers of the taigá.

May my flowers of the taigá,
reddest of the red, stand there
so their dreams will be untroubled,
not dreams about the camps.

I can hardly walk any more,
it looks as if I've had my days.
You build whatever you want to,
as long as it's not for evil.

The dam will flood my little home,
it'll disappear—well, let it go,
if only evil people
won't torture other folk . . ."

"Well, why are you silent, Granny?"
"Just so, dear boys, overcome . . ."
"But why are you crying, Granny?"
"Just so, it's nothing . . ."

And she blesses the excavators
and us,
with her thin, knotty peasant hand,
now and forever.

[1] Andrei Rublev (1360–1430) was a famous Russian painter
of icons.

Nushka

I am Nushka Burtova, I mix concrete.
I produce twice my daily quota.
Why are you staring at me like this?
You want me to tell you the story of my life?

I was born in 'forty-one,
on a mat in the fields, at harvest,
near an absurdly remote village in the taigá,
going by the name of Great Mud.

With her head drooping, as if confessing,
Mother lay emptied and serene,
and I was fastened by the navel cord
to her stiffening body.

Well, the women threw down their sheaves,
and bending over me, still alive,
they cut the navel cord with a sickle
and bandaged it with grass.

Froska, a neighbor, pushed her breast into my mouth,
Grandfather Nikodim wrapped me up—
in a faded banner that used to hang over the camp
with the slogan ALL FOR THE FRONT! . . .

And they laid me and my mother
on a sky-high cartload,
and there it was peaceful and soft for her,
and her sufferings were left down below.

And it never was known to her,
that almost a month later
a foolish bullet got my father
at Yelnya Town.

Our Chairman was not a peasant,
he came to our village from his lathe,
maimed in the Civil War,
his empty sleeve tucked into his pocket.
With his lonely hand he showed the death certificate
to the village meeting:
"People, how are we going to bring up this little girl?"
And the people answered: "We'll bring her up."

I was, in those bitter times,
a kind of unwanted, extra mouth to feed,
but nobody in our village
ever called me "orphan."

Hiding kindness under sternness,
the Chairman used to thrust at me, like a father,
carrots sometimes, then a rag doll,
then a sweet with tobacco stuck to it.

I was fed with potatoes by the women,
and as far as they could, they dressed me like their own,
and I grew up as the daughter of the village,
and I loved it as my mother.

The sounds of war ended, the shooting ceased,
the sun of our victory rose,
yes, but my new mother still suffered
and I could not understand why.

"Fulfill your plans!" they nagged from the town.
The telephone went mad with calls,
yes, but our hands kept squeezing for nothing
the dried-out teats of our cows.

War, you brought to our village
such sorrow, and want, and ruin,
but the hands of the peasant toiled
in the fields from dawn to dusk.

These hands, so precious,
they were coarsened, but somehow tender,
they made our Russia grow again
after that most cursed war.

And such hands, covered with cuts
and forever black from soil,
thrust onto me a crisp briefcase,
and sent me off to school.

Awkwardly we sat at our desks,
so timid we didn't dare to breathe.
The teacher smelled strangely nice—
I didn't know it was her perfume.
City-bred, wearing glasses, and a jacket,
she broke the silence and asked us:
"Tell me the meaning of Fatherland, children!
Well now, children, think it over, well . . . ?"

We were stuck, silent and ashamed,
no one had taught us this word.
"I know," Peter suddenly leaped up, triumphantly,
and stammered "Our native land."
"All right, but what about 'Our native land'?"
Impatiently she tapped with her pencil on the desk.
I thought immediately "It is our village!"—
but in panic I stayed silent in the corner.
I was learning, I was straining my brains,
I moved the pointer across the map.
I harnessed the sluggish horses,
I dragged them on by the leads.
I milled, chopped, weeded,
carted bushels to the granary,
filled chaff bags for the cows,
even though they couldn't eat it.

I would take a homemade basket,
and a resplendent painted box as well,
and go to the taigá for red bilberries,
for mushrooms, and for wild garlic.

From the taigá—my own garden—
I would hurry to the Chairman,
because among all the hungry villagers
he was the hungriest of them all.

He ate greedily, shoveling it all in at once,
and made jokes, to hide his anguish:
"We have mushrooms, but there isn't any cream . . .
We have bilberries, but there isn't any sugar . . ."

He would take an old photo of Lenin,
and stare at it for hours, smoking,
as if he was asking some question,
talking about something.

And then, suddenly coming to,
he would hug me firmly to his chest.
"Never mind, Nushka, it will all be changed . . .
just wait for a while, just wait . . ."

He darted between village and telephone,
always in a tearing hurry.
Demands for grain came in a frenzy,
from the village and over the phone.

Boars howled from hunger like wolves,
while the telephone shouted "You must fulfill the plan."
Then one day with his decrepit double-barreled gun
he shot himself in the heart.

And he lay there, and each one of us was ashamed
that we hadn't saved him from the trigger,
and shining on the lapel of his jacket
Lenin was frowning at us.

Both of them looked at us silently.
It was frightful for me and the others
that the lid of the coffin would slam down
over Lenin and over him.

I was growing up, finishing seven years' schooling,
but in my stuffy bunk in my sleep
I would shout heart-rendingly at times.
Something terrible I had dreamed . . .

And in the autumnal slippery bleakness,
from the village of Great Mud,
having received my passport at last,
I went into domestic service.

My master was a bigwig—
though he was neither reptile nor villain,
I felt without any doubt at all
he must have been one of those people on the tele-
    phone . . .

He treated me properly, didn't shout, didn't swear,
though it's true he never gave me a place at his table,
and on the festive day of the Eighth of March
he would shake my hand triumphantly.

And worn out by drink, he would speak, in his deep voice:
"Now, Nushka, bring us some mushrooms,
and give us a song . . . myself, I come *from the people* . . .
Give us a song of the people . . . Sing for the soul!"

From morning on I vacuumed curtains,
spread naphthalene on coats, fur cloaks,
polished the piano, on which
not a soul in this house ever played a thing.

In wooden slippery slippers
I rubbed the polish into the parquet,
and once I found behind a commode
a dusty, well-known portrait.

I asked what to do with the portrait,
if maybe I ought to throw it out—
but the master, lingering over his answer,
smiled: "Let it lie for a while . . ."

He read the newspapers, and crumpled them up,
became sullen and sulky:
"Well, well. That's no good. Soon
they'll limit the Party members' income."

He dug into the meat jelly furiously,
coming back from the kolkhoz at night:
"I only banged with my fist, you understand,
but already they say: 'Don't bang . . . !'"

And trying in vain to fall asleep,
he'd grumble, I don't know at whom:
"Democracy! it's getting out of hand . . .
It's a pity the boss isn't there . . ."

His face expressing approval,
and also, as it should be, slightly severe,
putting his glasses on,
he checked the speech someone had written for him.

And he phoned: "Ilusha, you're brilliant . . .
In general, I must say, it's really good.
Perhaps add a bit more folksy humor
and a couple of good quotations."

And the quotations were tossed in,
and the people's humor,
and mutton, and young chickens,
and cucumbers, and salmon.

Whom he did love, I don't know,
but I knew then it wasn't the people.
His driver, not a very sociable fellow,
had just the right name for him—"Phony."

I wore out my hands in the laundry,
then fled, I couldn't stand it any longer.
Just by chance I then took up the profession
of dishwasher in a railway dining car.

And I washed wine glasses and tumblers,
and scraped rump steak and brains off plates
all the way from Moscow to Vladivostok,
and from there all the way back to Moscow.

I polished plates and shone glasses,
while the countryside sailed by the window,
factories and cranes floating by,
tractors, airplanes and haystacks.

Inside I felt peaceful and clean.
I looked out, and as though in a dream
the meaning of that word "Fatherland"
unrolled like the Volga, outside my window.

In that fatherland, severe and preoccupied,
to lead the life of a louse was to steal
from the workers, from the Red Square,
from the village of Great Mud . . .

They used to approach me with certain phrases,
they used to be free with their hands . . .
If they got really nasty
I'd slap them on the cheek.

And at the table those bawdy faces went sour
and were immediately silenced.
Fundamentally people were good.
Everywhere people are good fundamentally.

But among those who were eating and drinking,
and watching the lights through the windows,
were some special passengers—
sharing some secret between them.

No one else looked at the stations like this,
and all the little things of life going by,
with famished, craving eyes
surrounded by dark circles.

They were returning, long-awaited,
all wasted away to grayness,
coming from Kolyma, Vorkuta, Magadan,
at last they were returning to their homeland.

Surely no one could forget, all of a sudden,
the guard-dogs and the camp numbers,
but there was faith in these people
and not only deadly anguish.

And what right did I have
to lose my belief in life, enter the darkness,
when these people, mute from breaking stones,
had not lost it in their camps.

And one time a crowd of young people got on,
in cowboy dress and leather jackets,
singing songs of the mists and the cedars
over the mighty river Angara.

The wheels were dancing on the rails,
the windows were lashed by the wind of the taigá,
and then somebody raised his glass of cider, amid laughter,
and proposed a toast to the writer H. G. Wells.

And a bespectacled, terribly learned fellow
explained to me then that H. G. Wells
was really a bourgeois writer,
and didn't believe in things like the Bratsk Station.

I came close to the table, shyly,
and asked, coming straight to the point:
"Won't you take me with you, lads?"
And the lads answered: "We will!"

And I found myself hailing the taigá,
together with our boisterous mob,
not at all feeling very mighty
as we crossed the mighty Angara.

Startled geese were calling.
Somewhere elks trumpeted in answer.
We stood happily, the inhabitants of Bratsk,
in Bratsk, which didn't exist as yet.

But the total of Nushka's belongings—
were a pair of down-at-heel shoes,
and a peeling nose, and freckles,
and not quite seventeen years.

There was also a plywood suitcase,
full of unimpressive rags,
but for safety's sake, a tiny
padlock kept guard over it.

But in our tent there was no mincing of words.
They declared, as we chewed our porridge,
that with locks on our suitcases
we would never build the Bratsk Station.

Guiltily I shrunk to a pebble,
and on going to work in the morning
I flung that cursed lock into the Angara,
and with it the lock from my soul!

Pines became my personal property,
the figures chalked on the boards,
and also the smiles, but the tears—
the tears I shared with my friends.

And when I was asleep, the dam
shone for me, built by me,
to the rumble of machines and animals,
the dam was my personal property, no one else's.

Like a small piece of ice, the sun scarcely glimmered.
The crowbar was altogether too big for me,
and the drips hung down in icicles
below my sniffling nose.

But I told myself: "Nushka,
you want to lie down, yes, but don't do it.
Though the frozen drops are hanging from your nose
you are your village's daughter . . . Hang on!

You are swaying . . . You are not well . . .
But you dig and you drill, without falling,
so that life will be better everywhere,
and in the village of Great Mud!"

The dreadful wind was thrashing me,
and when I no longer had any strength,
the Chairman appeared to me
as he used to talk to Lenin.

And again I drilled with a roar
and for one thing only I lived and breathed:
that the coffin lid wouldn't slam down
neither on Lenin nor on him!

And I believed not in words only,
nor in empty newspaper lines,
but I believed with my crowbar,
with my shovel, and with my pick.

And later I poured concrete
and acquired some social weight
I grew along with the town
and was formed together with the Bratsk Station.

But it seemed, as the spring brewed its spells,
that I had only to lay down the drill for a moment—
and I, weighing in fact almost nothing,
would part from the earth and take to flight.

And would fly in the sky, and fly,
seeing nothing concrete nor faces,
wanting something like this around me,
something like the sky and the birds.

But to my joy and sorrow,
at the time of the waters breaking up the ice,
there appeared in the spring, in the office,
an interesting young fellow from Moscow.

He was proud . . . didn't drink, didn't swear,
didn't look sideways at the girls,
interested in art. And as for his tie,
he wore it even to work.

I was trying to convince myself: "Now, don't be silly!
On his table, don't you understand,
silly girl, there's no one's photo
but that of a French actress called Brigitte."

And frowningly I looked into the mirror
and didn't have to dig in my pocket for words:
"Me with my smattering of knowledge . . . my figure so
    chunky
and my cheeks that are far too red . . ."

I went and bought elk grease at the chemist
to soften the skin on my hands.
I rubbed and I rubbed them, in secret
even from my intimate friends.

And putting up with the gibes of my tormentors
I touched only the surface of my soup,
and took to swinging that cursed thing
called a hula hoop.

And I read through book after book
and I drank vinegar to make my color pale—
but I stayed chunky just the same,
and my cheeks remained red just the same.

Am I to blame, that this epoch
didn't have any time for me,
that I grew up on black bread and spuds
and never thought about my figure?

My cheeks have their high color not from vitamins,
nor from lying leisurely on beaches,
but from the lashing of satanic blizzards,
from cold of more than fifty below.

You wouldn't have smiled like that,
you wouldn't have looked like that,
actress Brigitte, if you'd lived
in Nushka's skin even for a little while!

I am forcing myself to forget
but I'll never be able to forget
how on the May Day celebration
we sailed in boats into the taigá.

We drank home brew and ate fish and tomato,
we toasted love and the Bratsk Station,
already somebody had someone's lipstick on his cheek . . .
and somebody had already disappeared with someone
    somewhere . . .

As if nailed to one spot I watched him secretly,
far away from them all, myself included,
meditating by the fire, wrapped up in himself
with a tiny radio set in his hand.

A dance called the mambo floated over,
with the roar of Paris and London,
and I whispered: "Dearest Mamma,
if only he would look at me, just once!"

And he did look—at first curiously . . .
then he looked around—we were alone,
and nodding towards the fir trees in the evening,
he said (rather tiredly) to me: "Let's go . . ."

And I went, though I knew with a sick heart
that it was so easy because
I just happened to be handy, right near him,
and that French girl was so far away.

I shivered, like a tiny wild creature
from tears, and from the shame.
Goodbye, what used to be Nushka!
Goodbye, Good-b-y-e . . .

And I cried to myself . . .
He was frightened: "What's up?"
But Paris was laughing at me
from the radio by my side on the bed of needles.

From that time on that Muscovite got smart:
he selected new rosters for me
and ordered me new equipment,
and acted as though he hadn't noticed a thing . . .

But during my shift one day
everything on earth began to sway
and nudging inside me something
was announcing itself.

I was unwell more often,
almost couldn't look at food . . .
But why was I such a fool
as to tell him all about it?

He measured me with a cold, fleeting glance,
and fiddling with his little radio,
he mumbled: "Certainly I was the first,
but, you know, someone else could have been second!"

The slogans were battling it out as always:
THE SEVEN YEAR PLAN IN FOUR YEARS!
but I was fleeing, I don't know where,
from all my pain and grief.

I ran up onto the scaffolding
to finish myself off right away,
but I stood still like a statue
when I saw my Bratsk Station below.

And I was grabbed like a child,
with eyes full of defenseless reproach,
by the unfinished dam,
by its steel framework and its voices.

And through the wails of the sirens
and the confusion of blue welding arcs,
the Chairman and Lenin were looking at me,
and those people from the camps.

And my little village shouted
and my Angara shouted too:
"How can you do such a thing, Nushka?
How can you?" And I could not do it.

I hid my condition with difficulty
from the girls and the fellows in my team,
and on receiving the leave allowed me
in the ninth month I lay in the maternity hospital.

I was restless in bed at nights,
then, to the roar and flashes of Bratsk,
the new member of our community appeared,
floppy, and all soaking wet.

There he was, so indomitable,
clinging to everything, even though weakly.
There he was, quite blameless,
and roaring like the construction foreman!

And, Chairman, when giving him my breast,
I didn't shed any tears.
In your honor I named him Trofim,
though the name is not in fashion.

I sunk deep into motherhood,
but meanwhile in my ward
flowers and mandarins were arriving,
rattles, preserves, and jam.

Well, very soon a nurse with gray hair,
helping me into my coat,
told me: "They're waiting for you out there . . ."
And I swear I didn't know who it could be.

And, hugging my precious bundle,
and, I confess, hiding some anxiety,
swaying on my feet, which weren't too firm yet,
I saw the whole team before me.

And I started to cry, most unbecomingly,
leaning weakly against the wall.
I realized they had known it all along,
but they never let on to me.

Tears were flowing like a flood—such a shame! . . .
But snapping me out of my tears:
"Give us a look, how's our little son . . ."
said our foreman, rather abruptly.

They all helped me, as if they were my savings,
and from that time on I was always asked,
by the men from the assembly unit, or by the painters,
smilingly, "Well, how is our little son?"

And a cab driver, suddenly stopping,
would stick his head out of the cab,
even though he didn't know me at all,
smilingly, "Well, how is our little son?"

The excavator operators, the riggers
spoiled him, the rascals,
and in a confused way, but meaning well
they raised him like fathers.

And looking out with his clear blue eyes,
he could not yet understand
that he had become the son of the construction,
as his mother was the daughter of the village . . .

And among the huge crowd of my companions
a year later, I was marched with him to the band.
And this special day, happy and frightening
was the opening day of the Bratsk Station.

I whispered softly: "Troshka!"
hugging my son to my breast,
"I am going to cry, but only a little.
I am going to cry but you'd better look around . . ."

And it seemed to me that thousands were crying
and the waters were surging from the tears,
and the great light went up and on
through our veins and through the wires.

From the banners, triumphantly red,
Lenin was beaming down on people,
and the Chairman was probably standing
somewhere in the crowd, amid the bleached-out overalls.

And to music, to shouts and caps thrown in the air,
the Bratsk Station sparkled and roared.
It was a pity that the bourgeois writer Wells
was not also present at the opening . . .

And now, suspended with my workmate Svetka
on a rope ladder, at a crazy height,
putting the last touches of cementing
to the dam's gray back.

All, it seemed, was quiet, all going to plan,
but my hands gave a childish shiver
as I thought to myself: our little trowel,
its shape is like a heart.

I certainly won't go into details
of what the future is promising us,
but I am smoothing it with my heart,
so it will never crack.

So that women won't bear orphans,
so there will be enough bread for all,
so that innocent people won't be flung in jails,
so that no one will have to shoot himself ever again.

So that all in love will be honest
(and I am longing for love myself),
so that our communism will be achieved
not for self-seekers but according to Lenin.

I no doubt will die, though it's early
yet to be talking about that,
but I shall remain as light
for years, and maybe for centuries.

And at the factory, and in your study,
and in the most intimate circle of your family,
this you must know: those familiar electric lights
were Lenin's, and a little bit mine.

Let grandsons and granddaughters remember,
that this light, getting brighter and brighter
all the time, was inherited from Nushka
who came from the village of Great Mud.

The Bolshevik

I am the dam builder Karzev,
not one of those feeble old men on nerve tonics,
even though I'm past sixty, my boy.
Let us talk properly,
and pour, as you should if you're a man,
vodka in the tumbler, lemonade in the wine glass.

You'd probably like me to start right away
about our heroic exploits, wouldn't you?
But I'll begin again with fathers and sons.
You are young, but I perhaps was even younger
when, aflame with the world's fire,
I was cutting down all sorts of enemies of the Commune . . .

My roan horse flew, arching his neck,
knocking the crosses off the churches with his horseshoes,
and the wenches, shaking their necklaces, crowded around
me,
invitingly, but all to no purpose
while I, clad in sword belts, grenades and sheepskin hat,
wiped my sword on the cornflowers.

And I dreamed I saw Hindus in machine gun carts,
and Peruvians in helmets and leather jackets,
Berlin, Paris and Rome rising in rebellion,
the whole world wakened by Russia,
and Budenny[1] galloping across Africa
and I, of course, galloping after him.

And with my sword always recklessly ready
to slice off the Eiffel Tower
or smash to smithereens with hand grenades
the shopwindows of sausage-stuffed New Yorkers,
we came to the Komsomol Congress in ragged shoes
but with puttees made from a priest's chasubles.

I fidgeted: Why were they so slow announcing
the conflagration? Where, then, was Lenin?
"But there he is . . ." whispered my neighbor from Tver.
And I sighed: Now IT will happen.
But Lenin came in and he said: "Study,
study and study . . ." What's this?

But I believed in Lenin . . . And in my greatcoat
I went to workers' classes, and we hungry Young Communists
went out of our minds at lectures.
With Marx and Engels, productions by Meyerhold,
cheap cigs, Mayakovsky and pickled sprats.
They never gave us time to mope.

Arduously I gnawed away at the granite of hydro-construc-
tion.
I exposed alien tendencies,
branding with shame neckties and fox trots.
At debates I fought against Yessenin
for seeing only the little birch trees,
and not calling the people to industrial might.

There was NEP.² Bourgeois twitching to the two-step.
I bitterly remembered how the steppes were singing,
how the pale, tense sword blades
flew over the commotion of epaulets and stripes
reaching in flight right to the pampas
which, it seemed, were now so close.

Aspiring to heroic deeds, I did not at first understand
that NEP itself was heroic, and not a retreat.
And the true follower of Lenin, my boy, is he
who, if there's no bread and the cows are dying,
will have a go at anything, throwing dogma to the devil,
in order to feed the people, to save them.

Steam engines cried all over Russia,
tears froze to our shivering bayonets.

In streetcars, pilfering stopped.
Swaying, I walked to farewell Lenin,
and like a living thing, in my mitten
I kept my party card warm—like his.

And I whispered to the encircling snow storm:
"We shall tear Lenin away from death,
we shall tear him away from danger!
If there is a lie, we will tear him away from this lie!
Comrade Lenin, only let us wipe away our tears
and we will go into battle again, following you."

In Uzbekistan I built a dam . . .
Just imagine the beautiful picture,
with donkeys being used instead of trucks . . .
However, beckoning and dangerous
the reeds trembled uneasily
reminding me of those pampas in the Revolution.

We were tormented by the heat, shaken with malaria,
but that didn't matter, we were young.
We were holding our own, under the eyes
of the mountains, which, all in clouds,
from immense distances looked gloomily down on us
like counterrevolutionaries in quilted gowns.

Our hands serving for modern equipment,
we dug away with picks and hoes,
feeding on the winds and drinking birds' milk,[3]
and I was happy to fall onto my trestle bed.
And somewhere far away Mayakovsky shot himself,
(and later Meyerhold[4] was put in jail).

I was so thrashed out by the end of day,
that my skin was steaming. Terrible thoughts
burst into my head, gloomily, heavily.
Numbed and guilty
I couldn't understand what's going on—
my country seemed to live two separate lives.

In one I built power stations to the howl of jackals,
there was Magnitka, the Moscow Underground, and
    Chkalov,[5]
songs like "Arise, arise you curly head . . . ,"[6] and the
    storm
of applause over there in the Kremlin's hall . . .
In the other—sobs: "Father taken in the night . . ."
And the stars of my marshals were cast to the ground.

I needled my mates with my questions.
With Alyoshka Fedoseyev, the foreman, I
drank home brew made of currants,
and with his fist he threatened somebody:
"But all the same, we'll build the Commune!"
And, crying, he shouted at me: "Sshh! No tears!"

But our chief said to me, with the face of an ascetic,
that the Party is dearer than friendship with anyone.
He looked piercingly at me, adjusted his jacket,
and knocked significantly on the safe:
"There is material here—your Fedoseyev is an enemy . . .
Tomorrow there's a Party Committee meeting . . . think
    up a speech . . ."

"That's how it's got to be"—he couldn't help adding.
"That's how it's got to be!"—they said. And I used to fight.
"That's how it's got to be!"—and I studied, right from
    the beginning.
"That's how it's got to be!"—I built, not asking rewards,
but if they ordered me to lie, by saying, "That's how it's
    got to be,"
and if I so lied,
                    I would be a traitor to Lenin!

And I, hacking lies to pieces,
stood up for Lenin and for Alyoshka,
at the Party Committee meeting, as I had at Sivash.[7]
I took no notice that my chief was not disconcerted,
and furiously shook his bell
and violently tapped with his pencil.

I was called to Tashkent. I thought,
this was to clear up this low slander.
I was ferocious. I was still blind.
They came into my room for a short talk
and then took me away in a van, on which
as I remember, was written BREAD.

When those bastards tortured me,
and hit me in the face, and broke my arms,
and did such things to me—
my tongue couldn't manage the words to tell it—
and tried to buy me with: "A little drink?"
and thrust false confessions at me,
then I wheezed out just one thing: "I am a Bolshevik!"

They said to me, grinning: "All right!"—
shoved me onto a stool, a lamp in my eyes,
and the light lashed me, and was finishing me off.
My boy, don't forget this, ever:
taking it in turns, in front of Lenin's portrait,
those bastards tortured me with the very light
that I was seeking for happiness!

And I whispered to the portrait in a frenzy:
"Forgive us, forgive us, Comrade Lenin . . .
We shall conquer them in your name.
Even if things are bad, even if they get worse,
we shall not sell our souls, Comrade Lenin,
and we won't sell out communism either!"

In the taigá we felled timber, dumbly,
Party members, engineers, men of the Cheka,
divisional commanders . . . How could such things be?
Did you know, secret agents, whom you were putting away?
And to my horror, it seemed as if it was not people,
but communism itself, they wanted to imprison.

However, there were some foul reptiles even there . . .
I remember, rushing over from the haulage crew,
my former chief, clad all in rags, throwing himself at me.

But I answered him, not without tact,
"The Party is dearer than friendship. There you are!"
He kept away from me ever after that.

I became tougher and at the same time softer.
Suffering does enlighten us, my boy.
And how well I remember, sitting on some wind-felled
    trees
by a small fire, a Regional Committee man from Sverdlovsk
reading to us Yessenin's poem of the birch trees,
and I was ashamed of my earlier words about him.

War . . . I remember, Hitler started it so smartly . . .
But I, "Enemy of the People," built for our own victory
another power station in the Caucasus.
We chiseled it cunningly out of the rock,
with Heinkels bombing us at night,
though the snotty-nosed lot couldn't reach us!

Around us the guards stood, watching,
and you, Comrade Stalin, did not understand
that far from your guard,
we, the prisoners, given numbers by you,
were crossing seas and rivers,
and with the army reached Berlin.

Not one of us was called a hero,
no red banner fluttered above us,
but we fought for our native land
and closing our ranks, as if under the red banner,
we repulsed all sorts of Vlasovs, crooks
and other counterrevolutionaries, as if in battle.

Remaining, just the same, an "Enemy of the People,"
I built a power station on the Volga, and didn't give in.
They hid us from foreign eyes,
but we beat all records. We didn't give a spit
that no one photographed us, or painted our pictures,
or wrote feature stories about us.

But I was getting older, and the Volga soothed me,
whispering to me: "Not much longer . . ."
But not much longer what? To live? Stooped and gray,
I carried my burden, worn out,
until the Twentieth Congress put my Party card
back into my weakening hand.

I wouldn't say that my youth returned
at once on wings of happiness, no, no,
but I went out to build the Bratsk power station.
Yes, my boy, youth is irretrievable,
but look out the window; isn't that a dam there?
All right. That proves my existence.

I see you're a bit sad, my boy.
Here, ease your sadness with a pickled mushroom,
and have a drink, and pour one out for me.
Did I mention painful subjects? Well, I'm not sorry,
you have to be reminded . . . Well, in the meantime
I'll go on about fathers and sons.

You must remember, when you see the buildings and the
     dams,
what they did to me with my own light in the past.
Technical progress isn't everything, not at all.
Don't you forget that great legacy:
"Always towards the light!"[8] If there is no light in our souls
no power station will help us.

You must remember our fur hats with the stars,
and the pampas that were burning in our eyes,
the sleepless nights when we were building,
"I am a Bolshevik!"—under that cursed lamp,
belief in a life beyond the watery soup of that camp,
. . . don't dare in any way betray such fathers!

You must remember them all, those who cleared the land,
those who built, those who were heroes without any fuss,
who didn't save a penny for themselves.

You must remember the breed of commissars
who never lied to the people,
and you must never lie, my boy, never!

But remember other fathers too—ferreting out reports,
putting people away, or basely silent—
don't forget such fathers either!
Spit on their threats or on their kindness,
go ahead, my boy, honestly like those commissars,
set the truth of your fathers against such scoundrels!

And if you're ever in a tight spot
don't betray your conscience, nor your friend,
you'd be betraying the dead and the living alike.
Go, my boy! And when you're preparing for battle,
know that Alyoshka, Lenin and I are behind you.
And swear this oath: "I am a Bolshevik!"

---

[1] Simeon Mikhailovich Budenny (1883-   ), Marshal of the Red Army. Hero of the Civil War and of World War II.

[2] NEP was the New Economic Policy, which for a short period during the 1920s permitted a certain amount of capitalism in the Soviet Union.

[3] In Russian, the phrase "feeding on the winds" (lit. "air") means to have bad food or a shortage of food; in other words, life was so difficult that there was scarcely anything to eat. "Birds' milk" here is used as "hens' teeth" would be used in English, to mean "that which does not exist." In Russian, a phrase including this expression would usually be used to indicate abundance, almost superfluous luxury, thus giving its use in this context a nice irony.

[4] Vsevolod Meyerhold, director at the Moscow Art Theater whose expressionistic theater was suppressed in the middle 1930s.

[5] Valery P. Chkalov (1904-38), Soviet aviator, who flew from Russia to America over the North Pole.

[6] "Arise, arise you curly head" was a popular song of the period.

[7] Sivash, on the shores of the Sea of Azov, not far from Perekop, was the scene of a Civil War battle.

[8] "Always towards the light!"—allusion to Mayakovsky's poem "An Unusual Adventure."

The Light Controller

I am the light controller, Izzy Kramer.
I send out current to peasants and doctors,
move containers and mobile cranes
and spin the reels of movies.

Somewhere in the noiseless lanes
wandering couples embrace, as always.
Does Izzy Kramer light you up too brightly?
If so, I can dim it.

As for my private life, it's in a bad way.
Up to now there is no wife for me.
Forty isn't old, it's true,
but forty isn't young either.

I'm not sorry for my fate,
but why then, after all,
are my teeth of stainless steel
and my head as gray as can be?

Here I am at the control panel, over the water,
thinking of one thing and another,
but there are two of us in this wide world,
a fact that nobody knows.

I am here, and at the same time somewhere else.
Here, there is work, but there—corpses, corpses . . .
The barbed wire of the Riga ghetto
has torn me in two.

Both Izzies are under the same skin.
One is hot, the other shivers,
to one, the shout: "Good luck, mate!"—
to the other: "Hey, you lousy Yid!"

And from one, cities like children
born in the taigá, ask for light;
the other has a miserable yellow star
stuck to his sleeve.

But onto that one, onto his star and cap,
wild cherry blossoms could still fall.
Even in the ghetto seventeen is seventeen,
no matter what you say.

Greedily the body breathes through its rags,
asking something of the spring . . .
But Riva's hair is long and misty,
like a rabbi's prayer.

Drunken SS men are jeering,
loafing around the ghetto till dawn . . .
But Riva's eyes are like explosions,
black, with fire in them.

She prays, petrified,
but her lips don't want to pray,
flying to meet my lips,
just as inexperienced as hers.

And, forgetting death and hunger,
full of something special of our own
we went to a symphony concert
given in a warehouse.

A very small orchestra appeared,
breathing on their fingers as they came.
The SS had given permission
for Beethoven to be performed for the Jews.

The little old men, on plywood cases,
raise their fiddles, sickly,
and their frenzied bows dance
across our nerves, across our throbbing nerves.

And the blizzard of the bombing resounded,
choruses of dead women and children,
and then came in, rumbling like organ pipes,
the chimneys of the ovens waiting for us somewhere.

Your blood, Maydanek and Auschwitz,
flows from the piano's keys,
and, raging—German against German!—
Ludwig van Beethoven rebels.

Now a mob of SS men burst in the door on us,
reeking of recent drinking . . .
Poor genius, they used you for bait,
you who were blessed by God.

And again the soldiers are dragging us
off somewhere to torment and torture.
Ludwig van Beethoven, someone's hands
are tearing Riva away from me!

Birds bypass our concentration camp,
clouds sail far aside,
even the rats won't live in it,
but the people here try to survive.

I can't sleep, lying on my lousy plank bed,
and I have this one and only prayer:
"O God, don't torture Riva as I was,
rather let Riva die!"

But once, silently digging the earth
close to the women's camp,
I almost shouted . . . I could see Riva,
near me, like a ghost.

But there she stood, almost invisible
in her transparent, childlike thinness,
swaying like a wisp of the smoke
coming from the camp's brick chimney.

And I can't tell whether
she's alive or dead . . . like one sunk in a dream
lifeless she is stuffing mattresses
with human hair.

A German woman, hands on hips, is walking up and down,
looking on at this terrible work.
Her boots are squeaking, they shine painfully.
Brand new boots. Hurting her.

"Hey there, Yid girl, do you hear me, drop those mat-
    tresses!
Come here. Come on, give me a hand."
I weep. Riva is pulling the boots
off her stout German legs.

"Hurry up! Do you want the lash?
And don't tear my stockings!"—giving her a kick in the
    chest—
"And now stretch them for me, slut!
Put them on! Are they on? Now, get going, on the double!"

And she runs, Riva runs, round in a circle,
tripping over the stones,
and the soldiers, with their shiny snouts,
grin smirking down from the towers at her!

O my God, I begged you for her death, do you remember?
Why then is she still alive?
I cry out, reach forward to help her,
but a friend of mine stops my mouth.

And she runs, runs in a circle,
falling down, rising, her face bloody.
O my God, stretch out your hand to her,
stop her forever!

O my God, once more I beseech you!
Merciful God, this cannot be!
The sun, like the camp's searchlight,
strikes into Riva's senseless eyes.

She has fallen . . . her girlish, graying head
is pressed to the moist earth.
God has at last remembered pity.
God has heard, Riva! You are dead . . .

I am the light controller, Izzy Kramer.
I look at you with the lights of Bratsk,
rumbling with electric tractors,
whistling with electric trains.

Somewhere, at a Beethoven concert,
you are sitting, perhaps with your wife,
yes, and I—you won't be angry?—
sitting nearby, on an extra chair.

However, it isn't really me, but someone else . . .
Ludwig van Beethoven, I am now
lighting up the notes on the music stands,
from out of the taigá, wiping away the tears from my eyes.

And when you pay the light bill for your flat,
negligently stuffing the bill in your desk,
do remember the dreadful price
Izzy Kramer paid for that light.

Izzy knows: there's a great need for light,
so that neither you nor I will ever again see
the barbed wire of ghettoes,
nor yellow stars frozen to sleeves.

So that no one's sated laughter
will disgracefully jeer at Jews,
so that the word "Yid" will disappear forever,
not degrading the word "man."

This Izzy here is a man of importance—
the Angara is lying at his feet,
yes, but somewhere the other Izzy is weeping, weeping,
and Riva keeps on running, running . . .

The International

When *The International* is being sung
a purification takes place in me,
and on my lips
                    I have a feeling
as if I had kissed the banner . . .
The International
                    jets through me,
when at the Bratsk Station,
                              brother of brothers,
I see side by side
                    Russians,
                              Ukrainians,
Tatars,
        Jews,
              Chuvashes,
                        Buryats.
I believe only in struggle, not in prayers!
I foresee:
          the day of enlightenment, not so far off,
when, like the International Brigade at Madrid,
the peoples of the world
                          will unite.
I foresee a world
                    not impoverished by hostilities,
erecting an eternal cross over squabbles
where the brotherly, united labor of people
gives them light
                  from a Universal Bratsk Station.
In this Station,
                delivered from the past,
higher than anything on earth,
I foresee
        Russia
              together with a new Spain
                              and a unified Germany!

In this Station
           in one dining room,
remembering the old days with a smile,
will be an American docker
                 and bearded Cubans,
Israeli peasants
          and Arab fellahin.
Shine out, people!
         Give light!
               Give light!
                     Give light!
So that mankind will indeed be uplifted!
And the Angara's waves,
             prophesying this,
sing
   as they rush along
            The International . . .

Don't Die, Ivan Stepanych

Don't die, Ivan Stepanych,
don't die, don't die . . .
It's wrong of you to act like this,
forsaking your paternal land.

You, lying there in the Bratsk city hospital,
gray-bearded, by the window,
and all around you are nurses, syringes,
and whiteness, and whiteness.

You are surrounded with kindness and attention,
here in this spacious building,
but you are departing, Ivan Stepanych,
you are departing from yourself.

Ivan Stepanych, do believe in treatment . . .
Ivan Stepanych, don't hurry . . .
But the body is slowly getting lighter,
freeing itself from the soul.

And the earth, dark under your nails
draws your hands, draws,
by some elementary force,
to unite again with the earth.

You lived in the tiniest farmhouse
by the lower reaches of the Angara itself,
and from your youngest days
you knew the soil down to the last grain.

And the Angara was like the soil,
always known to you,
in all its severe laws,
in all its rapids and channels.

For a whole year, stubbornly
you held out against all the rumors
that a dam had been built across the river,
and that it was giving light to people.

But then, thinking hard, while
looking up at the winking red aircraft lights,
you put some things in your knapsack
and took your boat to the upper reaches.

And there you saw the dam,
and then you saw our Bratsk Station,
and frail, gray and white, quietly
you with your knapsack poked around everywhere.

Not heeding the calls and the jokes,
covered all over with cement dust,
in disbelief you touched the dam,
and you were convinced: it was real.

And suddenly everything swayed before your eyes,
and the dam began to move sideways,
and your heart, as if it had stumbled—
your tired old heart let you down.

And you fell at the turn of the road,
hands spread strangely . . .
"Up you get, Grandpa, what's the matter?"
said the driver, trying to lift you.

Don't die, Ivan Stepanych,
don't die, don't die . . .
it's wrong of you to act like this,
forsaking your paternal land.

When the soldiers were marching on Berlin
then, building up strength for the battle,
the porridge they boiled
came from buckwheat you had grown.

Doctors, I beg you, help him,
do try to rouse him again . . .
Conqueror of Berlin,
can't you conquer death?

Rockets flew in space,
and cosmonauts sat in them.
We even had their pictures on our matchboxes . . .
And they were eating your bread.

The geologist drinks condensed milk,
exploring far-off lands—
but that red-brown cow
was milked by your old wife.

And you also built Bratsk with us
when we were running the construction job here,
then your daughters dug
beetroot and potatoes for us.

Let all the people pass by the broad-limbed fir trees
walking behind his coffin,
and let the Government also walk behind him,
taking their hats off in silence.

And let people write
beautiful poems, erecting a cross
to the memory of Ivan Stepanych—
creator of the Sputniks and the Bratsk Station.

The Pumping Station

In the very heart of the Bratsk Station
climbing,
                almost like an acrobat,
                                        my eyes goggled
at the hatches and the machines.
But the freckled priestesses
of the temple of kilowatts
grinned into their mittens:
"The lad
        is not very strong!"
Felix was my good guide,
wise as a Hindu.
Without him I would have perished
by the hand of industry.
Felix poked his finger proudly
into each of the units:
"Do you feel?—
                That, my brother,
is technology—
                our ruler!"
And not blaming me for my ignorance,
in technical things my godfather,
he dragged me downstairs
to the pumping station.

This is automation—
                Yes!—
Wait till you see it,
one girl on duty, all alone,
merely as a formality!
Suddenly, all other sounds were stilled
by the howling from above

Felix proudly announced:
"We are
          under the Angara!"

My veins chilled,
I could scarcely keep calm,
while the pumps made shuffling noises
in the midst of the rumbling fog,
asking Felix
          as he held me by the elbow,
"What's the matter with him, has he had a shock?"
"Listen!" a whisper went through the shuffling.
The whisper
          breathed
                    to us:
"My darling,
          are you shivering?
My darling,
          don't be afraid.
My darling,
          come to me.
The night
     is before us.
My darling,
          pain throbs in the heart,
oblivion in the mind.
Take everything that is mine,
everything that is mine
                    is yours . . ."

The Angara
          pressed to me,
the darkness trembled.
"Everything . . .
          everything . . .
                    everything . . ."
Floating from all around me
"Everything . . .
          everything . . .
                    everything . . ."

Through the crash of the spray
"Everything . . .

            everything . . .

                        everything . . ."
Through the scream of machinery.
We went up the stairs, above,
into the hum of the giants of steel,
into the crackle of welding and the flying sparks,
into the grating

            crashes

                of noise.
Toppling waters

            raged.
Metal

      thundered.
Ah yes, but that whisper, rolling,
sweeping everything away . . .
Above the howling bridges,
above the great river,
above the shaggy taigá,

                above
technology, our ruler.

"Everything . . .

            everything . . .

                        everything . . ."
Rearing,

        drawing down,
"Everything . . .

            everything . . .

                        everything . . ."
Saying,

      flowing,
"Everything . . .

            everything . . .

                        everything . . ."
There, at the Bratsk Station.

"Everything . . .
                everything . . .
                                everything . . ."
somewhere in the sky.

Rising above the cranes,
                        as if hanging on a jib,
a lonely star
            was all trembling.
And I
    was drawn down to the water,
and now
        up to the star.
Felix said:
        "Wake up! Where do you think you are?"
I was everywhere.
That whisper
            had crushed me
torn me
        like an explosive,
and I had remembered something,
                            I called to it, remembering.
. . . It was a city all in red leaves,
but which one it was—
                    I have forgotten.
Maybe it was Paris?
Maybe it was Kharkov?
And a woman was running,
trembling from the heat,
not sparing herself,
her hair scalding red.
Through the fallen leaves
                        and scraps of newspaper
rushed her little heels.
Her body was bursting through the hooks of her dress,
her pupils
        through the whites of her eyes.
Houses were thundering to the ground,

and she whispered something
                    that sounded like
                                    "Mamma . . . Ma-mm-a . . ."

Drowning the thundering,
silencing the branches of the oaks,
"Everything . . .
                    everything . . .
                                    everything . . ."
trembled on her lips.
"Everything . . .
                    everything . . .
                                    everything . . ."
it is impossible to forget!
"Everything . . .
                    everything . . .
                                    everything . . ."
This cannot be killed!
"Everything . . .
                    everything . . .
                                    everything . . ."
cries and sings.
"Everything . . .
                    everything . . .
                                    everything . . ."
comes floating down the ages.

Shadows of Our Beloved

The ancient Greeks
                    had a builder's custom:
if you are building a house
                              then on a specially sunny day
you must
            stand the girl you love
                                       against the sun
and then you begin,
                     laying the first stone in her shadow.
And then your house won't crack,
                                  won't ever fall down.
Mountains will crash,
                       groaning,
                                  but it will be untouched,
and there will be no malice in it,
                                   dishonesty,
                                                greed,
                                                        envy—
the shadow of your beloved will protect
                                         this house from everything!

I don't know in whose shadow
                              the first stone of Bratsk
                                                         was laid long ago,
I can't see, builders,
                        but I'll take a closer look
where in the howling dam,
                           hiding quietly and sacredly,
are the shadows of your Natashas,
                                   your Zoyas,
                                               your Zinas and Marushas.
And you know, builders,
I have been building this poem, no easy task,
and on a cloudy day of my life

I laid down the first awkward line
in the shadow of my beloved,
                          of this complicated poem
in the shadow of my beloved,
                  as if in the shadow
                        of my conscience.

Shadows of our beloved,
                watch us, lest we retreat
                      into duplicity!
Recall us to our discomfort
              if we borrow experience
                  from comfortable untruth!
Don't let us retreat
          in the battle for revolution!
Show yourselves
     shining
           in the depth of the waves of red banners!
And when,
         although it is so difficult,
              we have built the Commune—
We won't be needing orchestras,
              speeches or rewards—
let them be there, like good angels,
          strictly,
             anxiously and youthfully,
the shadows of our beloved,
         keeping it safe.

A Crack

"A crack in the dam!"
The lads
            shudder.
They jump into cars
that come flying for them.
Alarm calls
                sound at the construction.
Guitars
        with ribbons
are flung
            onto beds.
Forget dances,
pictures!
Everyone
            like rioters
runs
    to the dam!
"A crack in the dam!"
Forgetting the toasts,
the wedding guests,
sober up at once.
The bridegroom runs
                        wearing a butterfly tie,
cursing
        his fancy clothes,
gathering speed
                    as he runs.
And his welder bride
                        pulling off her stiletto heels,
runs after him barefooted
                        in white
to the river's edge.
All those who a moment ago
                            were asleep

come together,
so the dam,
will be saved!

I live,
      not whining,
but at times
            I feel alarmed,
as I was that night.
The corrupt liar prattles
from the platform.
Siren,
      cry
the alarm!—
            A crack!
Maybe this crack
is just a tiny one,
not so ominous,
barely there,
but don't turn away,
don't be too late!
The danger is stealthy,
the danger is sly.
A woman is sobbing,
sick of being smirched . . .
Help! Hurry!
Alarm!
         A crack!
Someone's reputation is in danger . . .
Wake up,
         sleepy ones!
Jump
      into cars quickly!
Alarm—
         a crack!

Nature

We sailed in a launch to the town of Ustj-Ilim,
listing under the terrible wind,
and waves and stars were rolling,
breaking against us in spray.

And, spoiling us, like his own guests:
"Catch, you family of tramps!"—
a fisherman, swaying in a small boat,
hurled a catfish onto the deck.

And the cook, accepting the offering,
shouted to the seaman: "Right, full steam ahead!"—
and the wet night, under our searchlight,
twisted like the fish under his knife.

An owl laughed in the distance
and somewhere near a boulder
a lilac moon swayed
between the black horns of a reindeer.

And one of the water transport boys
rushed off in the middle of a shave
and grabbed me by the shoulders, pointing, "Nature!"
as if he'd created it all himself.

And if I was keeping dry, down in the crew's quarters,
relaxing in the morning—no show!
Like a goblin he tumbled down from the hatch,
"Up on deck! You'll miss the sunrise!"

And the sun seemed close to the exhaust pipe,
its light breaking against the stern,
like a pink mushroom
with pine needles stuck to it.

And a mother brown bear
looking at us not too cordially,
swam, white ripples breaking around her,
holding her cub in her teeth.

And the pines and the cliffs of cedars
were ruffled together in the scarlet haze . . .
"Nature!" exclaimed the helmsman
to all and sundry, and to himself.

Long ago, shaggy as animals,
blind from birth,
answering a mysterious call,
we came from the womb of the forest.

We are cutting it down, brutally,
when it is useful to us,
but all the same, when we want to be purified,
we go there, we go to the forest!

I know that nature embraces
the whole mysterious gamut:
Nature is the music of Mozart
as well as the iambics of Pushkin!

Forsaking nature, at times,
we wilt and waste away.
But our dams and our Sputniks
are part of nature, not something else!

Let the things made by our own hands
preserve us from growing senile,
let them deliver us from torments,
like the creations of nature.

So that, looking out onto constructions,
and curved bridges made by the hand of man,
we can simply breathe: "Nature!"—
and feel ourselves saved and clean.

Art

The fitter Slava Luchkin said to me:
"Now, lad, sit down and have a smoke!
There are better writers, I know,
but I like Saint-Exupéry.

And sometimes at night it seems to me
that this devil of a pilot is still flying,
gazing at us intently,
watching how we live."

We were silent in the twilight of the taigá.
It was still a long time till dawn,
and the Station twinkled like the anxious wing tips
of Saint-Exupéry's plane . . .

The foreman Spartak Sorokin
said to me: "I don't waste time on vodka.
In my view, we live in serious times
and I like serious music.

And throwing off my dirty shirt,
as soon as I come home from work in the evening,
I rush to Schubert and Bach,
Scriabin and Moussorgsky.

And I lie, while the record spins,
while standing stiff as puppies by the door,
my boots listen too,
covered with mud and cement . . ."

And one of the designers, Klava, said to me,
by a Siberian monastery:
"I have a bit of a treasure myself,
these thin little Skira books.

I see in the taigá the gardens of Gauguin,
the dove-colored haystacks of Cezanne.
Through the welders' sparks I see shimmering
the pale blue dancers of Degas.

Please forgive my fantasy,
but when the blizzard whistles
I see, covered in snow, Rodin's 'Thinker'
sitting on the edge of the dam . . ."

Art, you don't know yourself,
that on this distant shore
your light has dragged us from the swarms of midges
to the light of the future shining through the taigá.

We have made cliffs and trees fall down,
and ourselves fell down from weakness,
but Fellini, you came to us with your films,
traveling in the back of a dump truck.

Sharing all our afflictions with us,
Tolstoy walked through the raging snow,
Dostoevsky was tormented, restless,
Gorky walked with a child in his arms.

And not for nothing, but full of prophecies,
like the storm of thought,
Bratsk, you roar like Beethoven,
Bratsk, you thunder like Mayakovsky!

Mayakovsky

. . . And standing at the foot of the Bratsk Station,
I thought immediately of Mayakovsky,
as though he had risen before me, with his bony body,
his large eyes, resurrected in its tremendous presence.

Immense,
            awkward,
                        like the dam,
he stands right across all lies,
worn-out with work,
                        boiling over,
                                    devoted to the Party,
crushing squeals
            with thunder.

I can imagine
            how he would have hammered all phonies
with the weight of his lines,
swaying the taigá with his deep bass
as he read his poems to the builders.
You can't measure him with our own measure,
and in pain and numbness
I can imagine it all—
                  but Mayakovsky
in '37
      I can't imagine.
What would have become of him
if that revolver
            hadn't gone off?
                        If he had lived?
Would he have become more moderate, maybe?
            Would he have become more orthodox?
Would he have surrendered
                  to what he hated?

Would he have glumly stepped aside,
kept silent,
                gritting his teeth
                            from a distance,
when somewhere in the night,
                            in Black Marias
Bolsheviks were taken for execution?
I don't believe it!
Inflexibly,
            botheringly
he would have risen, flinging
                            his prophetic thunder.
Being dead, he has become
                            "The best
                                and most talented"[1]—
alive
    he would have been declared an enemy of the people.
And if that shot
                hadn't rung out,
not seeking for himself reward and fame,
like so many—
            he would have remained honest,
dragging the epoch on his shoulders.
No,
    he wouldn't have yielded,
                            wouldn't have broken—
he, like a spearhead
                    would have led us forward.
With all his life
                Mayakovsky calls us
to battles
        and not to suicide.
Although that shot is not fully explained, did he mean to
give us an example, shooting at himself?
That revolver fires again,
                            roaring with thunder
rising over the century—
that revolver,
            tested for durability,

from the past,
                    as if it were only two steps away,
fires into stupidity,
                    hypocrisy,
                                    banality,
enemies that are genuine,
                    not invented.
He teaches against lies
                    still stagnant,
to stand for the cause of the Revolution.
Mayakovsky left us cartridges in it,
so we could fire,
                    fire,
                            fire,
                                fire.

¹ "best and most talented." Words used by Stalin about
Mayakovsky.

The Graduation Ball

A ball,
        a ball,
                a ball in Red Square!
A full blast ball—
                the graduation ball!
Dear Granny, you're restless,
                        Granny, you're crying—
your granddaughter, Granny,
                        has already lost her high heels.
Her dress is split somewhere,
her beads
        are in the mud,
and your granddaughter has climbed
onto the place of execution.
Where you stood,
                Stenka Razin,
alongside the executioner,
a student girl
is dancing
        the cha-cha-cha.
Cider bottles,
                guitars and transistors
make up an orchestra,
                        with stamping and clapping,
and Red Square is dancing,
twisting and whistling—
as if antichrist had descended
                        —or Christ had risen.
The pale-faced voluntary militia
look on,
        shivering,
while youngsters in tight blue jeans
                        get
                        with it.

The bald-headed television newsman,
is practically dropping,
when he begs:
                    "Friends,
please,
        give us a waltz!"
But whistles
            and more whistles
follow such timid requests,
while his friends dance
the twist,
            the twist . . .

The engineer from Bratsk
wanders amid the festival,
looking a bit unsociable,
with his gray hair bristling like a hedgehog.
The boys are itching to dance,
dance and sing,
they don't realize it's Petka,
Petka in his hooded cap.

"Why,
        don't you like the twist?"
"No,
    it's not that at all—
I was simply remembering
a few other things . . ."

Without any urging
he can see
the boys from Magnitka
and their concrete.

The boys dancing on the concrete,
five forelocks flying, tipsy.
The boys dancing
like mad country wine makers.

Their starred, hooded caps,
leaping, dancing—
the dance of the childhood of industry,
the dance of their own youth.

The ball,
        the ball,
                the ball in Red Square!
Petka looks on from the past,
                        from under a graying head.
"Even though your dance is strange
                        you dance it well—
Only don't forget
            how we danced before . . ."
A girl à la Brigitte
laughs ringingly;
somewhere Sonka
lies still.

. . . Why are you so strangely silent, Sonka?
Why don't you get up?
Her slim International card[1]
pierced by a kulak's knife . . .

That concrete, boys,
                we mixed it for you,
and for that very reason,
                our enemies wrought vengeance on us.
You with stiletto heels
                and moccasins,
don't forget Sonka's broken-down boots . . .

The changing of the guard:
laughter dies down.
They head off for Lenin's mausoleum
as if swept by the wind.

The boys and girls
look how the guards

march,
with measured steps.

Grow up clean and high-principled,
young generation,
or else Sonka won't forgive you,
nor will Lenin!

The Commune calls you to battle!
Leave your childhood behind you,
get ready to relieve the guard
by Lenin's doors!

[1] Card of the International Society for Aid to the Soldiers of
the Revolution.

In a Moment of Weakness

When
        phony trickery
                        with a stupid air of prosperity
offends my gaze,
I wish
        I could retreat to the virgin forest,
somewhere,
                even to the Indians.
But there aren't any virgin forests.
The Indians
            have long died out.
And my heart is tormented with longing
                            like a calf for the udder.

But it is shameful,
                I swear,
                        to lament
that there are so many dregs,
                        to talk about.
It is shameful
            to hide oneself
                        from the present day—
We
    should
        remake it!

There are different ways to hide:
Some hide themselves in roars of laughter,
                                some in whining,
some hide in petty routine,
some in large lies.
Some hide in hectic activities,
in dancing,
            football,
                    drinking,

in fishing
       and telling stories,
in card games,
          and dominoes.
Some hide themselves,
           like children,
in their cars and weekend cottages,
in tape recorders,
         in stamps,
in the office,
     their friends
         and their family.
But it is shameful—
        I shout it aloud—
to hide even in nature,
even in immortal books,
even in love and work.
I know
   how difficult our epoch is,
how hard to understand,
but if there is something wrong with it,
then we shouldn't hide—
        but fight!
Not fight singlehanded,
but together with all people,
together with the workers of Bratsk,
with physicists
      and wheat growers!
And when I am tormented with doubts,
seeking
   their cure,
I go
  like those envoys
        to Lenin,
I go
  like those envoys
        to Lenin . . .
I have seen many countries.

Of one thing
        I am firmly
                convinced:
Universal destruction
            or universal brotherhood
                    awaits us.
In my most terrible moments
I believe,
        as in redemption,
that all suffering mankind
will unite
        in Lenin.
Through wars,
            through crimes,
but nevertheless without turning back,
humanity goes forward
            to Lenin,
humanity goes forward
            to Lenin . . .

The Night of Poetry

The sun creaked on the hook of a crane,
going down into the depths of the rushing Angara.
The Station stood, growing darker on the right,
yet all in the sunset on the left.
It played with the stormy Angara,
creating magic from the water,
letting it in from the right, darkest of dark,
releasing it from the left all golden.
And we were happily startled,
snatching the wind in gulps with our teeth,
as we flew on the snorting, galloping launch
towards the Sea of Bratsk, ahead of us.
Everything glowed scarlet . . . above the scarlet waves
leaped the scarlet salmon,
and there before us was the sea,
in the green cradle of its mother, the taigá.
The sea played with the sparkles of fish,
with buoys and the willows by the shore,
and amused itself—truly, like a child
with a rattle—with our launch.
And leaning on the hand rails, hushed,
with shining eyes, like fathers,
because this sea was their child,
stood builders, dogmen, foremen.
And a slim woman whispered,
quite forgetting decorum among us all,
leaning her cheek on the captain's vest:
"Ah Paul, my Captain, what a paradise!"
And he embraced her with a tattooed hand,
while with the other one he held the wheel . . .
"Man and wife . . . they both are poets . . . !"
a redheaded sailor explained to me.

I observed this strange pair
of poets . . .

Paul was no longer young,
but he had eyes like Yessenin, and his gray forelock
fell turbulently over them, like a boy's . . .
And she also was not so young . . .
Escaping through the comb on the crown of her head,
gray showed here and there
through the color of her permanent wave.
And the skin of her hands, red and heavy
like the hands of all women who often do laundry,
was cracked . . . But girlish, lively gestures
would suddenly break through in them.
And with happy confusion in her eyes,
as if she had dressed herself up,
she pointed out the pale moon to her husband,
and sighed quietly, "Wish on the new moon . . ."
The launch was moored to the shore, and Paul,
authority in his voice, said: "We'll stop here."
Some carried brushwood, some put up tents,
some were already opening bottles.
It was dark.
                    Behind the lacework of stars and branches
the unseen Angara was sounding.
Thick soup was clucking in the pot,
                        and the red wings of the campfire
leaned out on the damp wind.
One of the seamen, a cheerful fellow
                            called Serenka,
unfolded his accordion (a wartime prize),
tightened the strap on his shoulder,
                        glanced
                            seriously around him,
winked, and sliced through the silence.
He shook his curly head at times,
then jumped like the devil on one leg,
popping up like a mushroom lifting the pine needles
in the sullenly watchful taigá.
We tossed the empties into the grass
and moved in closer to each other,
and the needles that fell into the vodka

only made it tastier.
And I began to feel myself once again,
I breathed, thawed out, felt light
and clean and free
and all my troubles far away.

Then I was asked to read, and again
I felt deep inside me somewhere
the lack of something fundamental,
that these people needed and I did not have to give.
I took pains, trying to select something,
from my poems spread about on view.
                          But it wasn't easy to select.
Well, to be precise, it didn't measure up
to these faces, these pines and the campfire.

Now Serenka, to the rustling of the pines,
sadly resting his forehead on his instrument,
his fingers touching the keys,
asked me, in the usual way:
                          "Do you want a waltz?"[1]
I didn't understand him, and he in answer
sighed, and played a few bars,
                          seeming a bit offended:
"I thought all poets liked to read
to music, like our Pashka . . ."
I read something . . .
                    Then Paul came out,
glanced around him, haughtily, darkly,
adjusted his seaman's belt with its anchor,
tossed his forelock and nodded: "Tango!"
And frowning he began to read . . .
                          looking straight through
us all, swaying heavily, as if in a storm.
His hand pulled at his torn vest
so that tattooed mermaids showed through the holes.
"Forget me, kinsmen, children!
Forget me, grumbling wife!

I am young! At dawn I will go
where my radiant love awaits me.
And I will buss her on the grass
and make her wreaths of orchids,
and our heralds, the May beetles,
will trumpet our love abroad.
Above us no frowning clouds,
no scorpions in our path,
and the asters in white headdresses
will follow us like maids in waiting!"
And we remained silent, kindly, blissful,
smiling timidly and brightly.
"Well, how was it—hot stuff?"

> asked Serenka in triumph.

And I sincerely answered: "Hot stuff!"
Meanwhile his "grumbling wife"
didn't grumble at all at his attacks,
but stirred the thick soup and was silent,
lost in her own withdrawn world,
listening to something inaudible to us,
looking at the crackling pine logs.
But Paul, with a sweep of his hand, cried: "Maia,
what are you doing sitting there? Read us something of
    yours . . ."
And Maia, for some reason taking off her earrings,
looking so fragile and small beside him,
entered the circle, and timidly stood in the middle,
then nodded to the waiting Serenka:
"Suffering."[2]

> And quietly she began:

"My lovely eyes, my lovely eyes,
I know not why I blame you.
A cruel stepfather tried to force my tears,
then hunger, and then war.
Then my faithless husband tried to force them,
and it seems to make his heart grow gay
if I cry from my torments now.
My lovely eyes grow heavy with yearning,
beautiful no more, just plain eyes,

and no one takes pity on me,
even if my tears turn into gold . . ."

Her husband muttered, a homemade cigarette in his lips,
obviously hiding a creative envy,
"No way out . . . and it isn't true about me."
But Maia said: "Well, I'll read something with a way out."
And standing in front of the fire near a precipice,
Maia, shining in the light,
raised her eyes to somewhere in the stars,
and gesturing to the Angara, began:
"My Angara, beloved Angara,
where are you running, wait for me!
Paler than a burnt-out candle
I stand above your haze of blue.
Do you remember a lad called Pashka?
He could swim so far.
He would twist your lilies, Angara,
into my plait[3] scented by you.
So much golden sand
poured into my shoes!
Oh how often we kissed,
but never enough for me.
Where are you now, my fashionable shoes,
where are you now, my plait as fresh as dawn?
My youth has run away
like a goat with its little peg.

My Angara, beloved Angara,
how much do you bestow on us!
Whiter than embroidery,
the mist that hangs over you.
There are firs and pines hanging over you,
and the clever eyes of little brown bears.
And little fish swim in your waters
shining like tiny little suns.
And there are ducks flying, and little ducklings,
and a thousand chattering birds.
Ah, but my lips that used to laugh

long ago, are silent now.
I was like a mischievous squirrel,
but my teeth are all cracked now!
I am like a cedar cone,
but all the nuts have fallen out!

My Angara, beloved Angara,
foretell a happy fate for me.
I won't forget to send a gift,
only give me back my youth!
Across you there is now a dam,
and above it floats a banner of red.
Quietly I will swim towards the dam,
and this is what I will say:
Dam, you must let me in,
in with the raging water;
dam, you must let me out,
the youngest of young again.
Dam, over the mountains
and over the forests, shine, shine!
Dam, take, o take away,
all the wrinkles from my face . . ."

You wanted to read something "with a way out"?
I have understood you, Maia . . . The way out
is that light, which we create ourselves,
which will illuminate us, clarify our souls.
And I thought also about our craving
for poetry . . . Oh, how many clear souls
are drawn to it, and not just those stilyagi[4]
not only "crowds of hysterical women!"
And false, empty lines are shameful
when everywhere—even by campfires like this—
almost all of Russia reads poems
and almost half of Russia writes them.
I remember, in Moscow one night, in a taxi,
taking the world in through tired eyes,
an elderly taxi driver, puffing quietly,
read his verse to me, without a break:

"Life went by . . . The merry-go-round closed down . . .
Now I don't know what to do.
I could be you, Sergey Yessenin,
not to write your poetry—but to take your place in the
noose!"

So let them write, write, however pockmarked their style—
to show them an arrogant, frowning face, would be truly
sin,
and if we have the smallest God-given gift,
then we must write on behalf of all, for all!
In what is called a wild mania of writing,
Russia is bursting with suffering and loving,
secretly, quietly or with a loud voice,
forced to express it, and so to express herself!
This is the way I was thinking, and at the end of our
holiday
we were singing the old songs
and many other songs too—yes, all sorts,
and that one "Do Russians really want a war?"[5]
And a Bulgarian named Tsanev
with eyes like Robespierre piercing the gloom of the black
taigá,
growing pale and aflame,
read us his furious vers libre:
" 'Do I really live?'
'Certainly . . .' Darwin reassures us.
'Do I really live?'
'I don't know . . .' smiles Socrates.
'Do I really live?'
'You have to live!'—shouts Mayakovsky
and offers his weapon to me,
so that I can find out if I really live."

Around us the pines droned in a frenzy
and the rain hissed, as it drizzled onto the coals,
and closing ranks as in a charge,
we all began to sing, led by Marchuk's guitar:

"But if suddenly some day
                    I shall fall,
no matter in what new battle
                    then shattering the world,
I shall fall just as if it was falling
                    in that distant civil war,
and commissars in dusty hooded caps
will bow silently over me . . ."
And they appeared to me as in the song,
in front of me—as how many times before!—
the commissars standing in those dusty caps
gazing intently at us.
There, like the command of Russia itself
not to barter ideals for words,
Pushkin, and Tolstoy, and Lenin, looked at us,
and Stenka Razin's crazy head.
They looked severely, immutably,
and I could hear the Bratsk Station roaring
in the grandeur of reason, over
the false grandeur of the Pyramid.

And through the mist, through the pine branches,
seeing its lights, like the light of the future,
all of us were the answer to the Pyramid,
and this light was also our answer.
I am happy I was born in Russia
with Stenka's crazy head.
In the Bratsk Station, Russia, your motherly image
shimmeringly unfolded itself to me.

You, bent so many years under the lash,
hungry, barefooted and naked,
you went through sufferings in the name of light,
and by suffering you earned the light, like love itself.

There are still too many slaves in the world,
and not all the overseers have vanished yet,
but hate is always powerless
if love, instead of contemplating, fights.

No fate is purer and more exalted,
than to sacrifice life without thought of fame,
so that on earth all men will have the right
to say to themselves: "We are not slaves!"

> Bratsk—Ustj-Ilim—Suchanovo—Senezh—
> Bratsk—Moscow

> 1963–65

---

[1] It is a custom in Siberia for people to compose poetry (either writing it down or improvising), and deliver it to a musical accompaniment.

[2] "Suffering" is a Russian ballad.

[3] Plait—It is customary for unmarried women to wear a single plait which after marriage is divided into two.

[4] The "stilyagi" are the Soviet equivalent of teddy boys.

[5] "Do Russians really want a war?"—poem by Yevtushenko, now a popular song.

OTHER NEW POEMS

Sleep, My Beloved . . .

The salty spray glistens on the fence.
The wicket gate is bolted tight.
                         And the sea,
smoking and heaving and scooping the dikes,
has sucked into itself the salty sun.
Sleep, my beloved . . .
                    don't torment my soul.
Already the mountains and the steppe are falling asleep,
and our lame dog,
                    shaggy and sleepy,
lies down and licks his salty chain.
And the branches are murmuring
                              and the waves are trampling
and the dog and his day
                         are on the chain,
and I say to you whispering
                         and then half whispering
and then quite silently
                    "Sleep, my beloved . . ."
Sleep, my beloved . . .
                    Forget that we quarreled.
Imagine—
      we are waking.
                         Everything is new.
We are lying in the hay,
                    We sleepyheads.
                              Part of the dream
is the scent of sour cream, from somewhere below, from
   the cellar.
Oh how can I make you
                    imagine all this,
you, so mistrustful?
                    Sleep, my beloved . . .

Smile in your dream.
    Put away your tears.
Go and gather flowers
     and wonder where to put them,
burying your face in them.
Are you muttering?
    Tired, perhaps, of tossing?
Muffle yourself up in your dream
     and wrap yourself in it.
In your dream you can do whatever you want to,
all that we mutter about
     if we don't sleep.
It's reckless not to sleep,
     it's even a crime.
All that is latent
    cries out from the depths.
It is difficult for your eyes.
     So much crowded into them.
It will be easier for them under closed eyelids.
Sleep, my beloved . . .
     What is it that's making you sleepless?
Is it the roaring sea?
    The begging of the trees?
Evil forebodings?
     Someone's dishonesty?
And maybe, not someone's,
    but simply my own?
Sleep, my beloved . . .
    Nothing can be done about it.
But no, I am innocent of that accusation.
Forgive me—do you hear!
    Love me—do you hear!
Even if in your dream!
    Even if in your dream!
Sleep, my beloved . . .
    We are on the earth,
flying savagely along,
    threatening to explode,

and we have to embrace
            so we won't fall down,
and if we do fall—
            we shall fall together.
Sleep, my beloved . . .
            don't nurse a grudge.
Let dreams settle softly in your eyes.
It's so difficult to fall asleep on this earth!
And yet—
      Do you hear, beloved?—
                  Sleep.
And the branches are murmuring
                  and the waves are trampling
and the dog and his day
                  are on the chain,
and I say to you, whispering
                  and then half whispering
and then quite silently
                  "Sleep, my beloved . . ."

The City of Yes and the City of No

I am like a train
                    rushing for many years now
between the city of Yes
                    and the city of No.
My nerves are strained
                    like wires
between the city of No
                    and the city of Yes.

Everything is deadly,
                    everyone frightened, in the city of No.
It's like a study furnished with dejection.
In it every object is frowning, withholding something,
and every portrait looks out suspiciously.
Every morning its parquet floors are polished with bile,
its sofas are made of falsehood, its walls of misfortune.
You'll get lots of good advice in it—like hell you will!—
not a bunch of flowers, or even a greeting.
Typewriters are chattering a carbon copy answer:
"No—no—no . . . No—no—no. No—no—no."
And when the lights go out altogether,
the ghosts in it begin their gloomy ballet.
You'll get a ticket to leave—like hell you will!—
to leave the black town of No.

But in the town of Yes—
                    life's like the song of a thrush.
This town's without walls—
                    just like a nest.
The sky is asking you to take any star
                    you like in your hand.
Lips ask for yours, without any shame,
softly murmuring:
                    "Ah—all that nonsense!"

And in no one is there even a trace of suspicion,
and lowing herds are offering their milk,
and daisies, teasing, are asking to be picked,
and wherever you want to be, you are instantly there,
taking any train, or plane, or ship that you like.
And water, faintly murmuring, whispers through the years:
"Yes—yes—yes. Yes—yes—yes. Yes—yes—yes."
To tell the truth, the snag is it's a bit boring at times,
to be given so much, almost without any effort,
in that shining multicolored city of Yes.

Better let me be tossed around—
                    to the end of my days,
between the city of Yes
                    and the city of No!
Let my nerves be strained
                    like wires
between the city of No
                    and the city of Yes!

Picture of Childhood

Elbowing our way, we run.
Someone is being beaten up in the market.
You wouldn't want to miss it!
We put on speed, racing to the uproar,
scooping up water in our felt boots
and forgetting to wipe our sniffles.

And stood stock-still—In our little hearts something
                                        tightened,
when we saw how the ring of sheepskin coats,
fur coats, hooded coats, was contracting,
how he stood up near the green vegetable stall
with his head pulled into his shoulders from the hail
of jabs, kicks, spitting, slaps in the face.

Suddenly someone from the right by the handcart
                                pushed his teeth in,
Suddenly someone from the left bashed his forehead with a
                                        chunk of ice.
Blood appeared—and then they started in, in earnest.
All piled up in a heap they began to scream together,
pounding with sticks, reins,
and linchpins out of wheels.

In vain he wheezed to them: "Mates,
                you're my mates—what's the matter?"
The mob wanted to make a job of it.
The mob were quite deaf. They were raging.
The mob grumbled at those who weren't putting the boots
    in,
and they trampled something that looked like a body
into the spring snow that was turning into mud.

They beat him up with relish. With ingenuity. Juicy.
I saw how skillfully and precisely

one man kept putting the boots in,
boots with greasy tags on them,
right under the belt of the man who was down,
smothered in mud and dungy water.

Their owner, a guy with an honest enough mug,
very proud of his high principles,
was saying with each kick: "We won't let you get away
    with it!"
booting him deliberately, with the utmost conviction,
and, sweat pouring, with a red face, he jovially called to
    me:
"Come on, youngster, be in it!"

I can't remember—how many there were, making a din,
                                beating him up.
It may have been a hundred, it may have been more,
but I, just a boy, wept for shame.
And if a hundred are beating somebody up,
howling in a frenzy—even if for a good cause—
I will never make one hundred and one!

Perfection

The wind blows gently, fresh and cool.
The porch is fragrant with damp pine.
A duck stretches its wings wide,
having just laid its egg.

And it looks like a faultless girl,
having laid in God's design,
a perfection of white roundness
on an altar of straw.

And above the muddy, thawing road,
above the moldering roofs of the huts,
the perfection of the disc of fire
rises slowly in the sky.

The perfection of the woods in spring
all shot through by the dawn,
almost disembodied, shimmers in mist
like the breath of the earth, all over the earth.

Not in the frantic shapes of new fashions,
not in shapes borrowed from others—
perfection is simply being natural,
perfection is the breath of the earth.

Don't torment yourself that art is secondary,
destined only to reflect,
that it remains so limited and lean,
compared with nature itself.

Without acting a part
look to yourself for the source of art,
and quietly and uniquely
reproduce yourself just as you are.

Be reflected, as a creation of nature
bending over a well
draws the reflection of its face
up from the ice-ringed depths.

The First Presentiment

TO V. KORNILOV[1]

The first presentiment of a poem
in a real poet
is the feeling of sin
committed somewhere, sometime.

Even if that sin was not his—
he considers himself guilty,
his navel connects him
to all the tribes of mankind.

And no longer his own master
he runs away from glory and ecstasy,
with his head ready to admit guilt
but nevertheless held high.

The casualties of war and peace,
every broken branch,
build up in him a feeling of guilt,
his guilt, not just that of the age.

And his life is frightful to him—
he feels it as sinful as sin itself.
Every woman—is his guilt,
a gift which cannot be returned.

Shame always moves the poet,
thrusting him into boundless space,
and he builds bridges with his bones,
paying what is unpayable.

And there—and there, at the end of his path
which is there, and cannot be escaped,

he will say: "God forgive me . . ."
not having any hopes that this will be so.

And his soul will part from his body,
and descend to hell, indifferent to paradise—
forgiven by God, but never
forgiven by himself.

---

[1] Vladimir Nikolayevich Kornilov (1928–   ), a Soviet poet, was born in Dnyepropyetrovsk, the son of an engineer. After study at the Gorky Institute of Literature in Moscow, he published first poems in 1953. His first book, *Pier,* came out in 1964.

Early Illusions

Early illusions are beautiful,
Early illusions are wounding
But what does it matter! We are above vanity,
we embrace the highest knowledge,
saved by our happy blindness.

We, who are not afraid of taking a false step—
fools, from the common point of view—
still keep enchantment in our faces
through all the disillusioned crowd.

We are driven towards the distance
                by a glimmering of something,
away from the daily grind, the calculations of everyday
    living,
from pale skeptics and pink schemers,
transforming the world with our reflections.

But the inevitability of disappointments
makes us see too clearly . . . On all sides
everything suddenly takes shape,
all unknown to us till now.

The world appears before us, unhazed; unmisted,
no longer radiant with something priceless,
but with all this truthfulness unmasked
as deceit. But what is gone—
                was no deception.

You see, it is not the knowledge of the serpent,
it is not the doubtful honor of experience,
but the ability to be enchanted by the world
that reveals to us the world as it really is.

Suppose someone with illusions in his eyes
flashes past, pursuing some distant gleam,
then it doesn't seem to us that he is blind—
it seems to us that we ourselves are blind.

A Sigh

He is reserved,
            my friend,
                        he is terribly reserved.
He is driven inward on himself,
the lid has shut down on him,
on the dark depths of his sadness,
                        like a well,
and his thoughts are bashing against the lid
and his fists are smashed by it.
He won't tell his troubles to anyone,
he won't sob them out in a rush,
tonelessly everything piles up in him,
and I am afraid
            there will be an explosion.
But there is no explosion,
            only sigh
after sigh—
    like a peasant woman burying her tears in a haystack,
like the convulsive sob of the sea
against the dusky, wet boulders.

I used to be so open, completely open,
I didn't hold myself back from anything,
and for that I was ditched by fate
as though by a mocking woman.
And I'm tired.
            I have become reserved.
I've stopped being trusting.
At times when I've been drinking
I catch myself at the point of explosion,
but there is no explosion,
                only a sigh
and another sigh,
    like a peasant woman burying her tears in a haystack,

like the convulsive sob of the sea
against the dusky, wet boulders.

My old friend,
            my unsociable one,
let us sit down, as before.
Let us fill up glasses to each other,
to sigh—
            now together . . .

Fury

They tell me,
          shaking their heads:
"You should be kinder . . .
                    You are somehow—furious."
I used to be kind.
            It didn't last long.
Life was breaking me
            hitting me in the teeth.
I lived
  like a silly puppy.
They would hit me—
                    and again I would turn the other cheek.
I'd wag my tail of complacency,
                    and then, to make me furious,
someone chopped it off with a single blow.

And now I will tell you about fury,
about that fury
            with which you go to a party
and make polite conversation
while dropping sugar into your tea with tongs.
And when you offer me more tea
I'm not bored—
            I merely study you.
I submissively drink my tea from the saucer,
and, hiding my claws,
                stretch out my hand.

And I'll tell you some more about fury.
When before the meeting they whisper:
                        "Give it up . . .
You're young,
            better you write,
don't jump into a fight for a while . . ."

Like hell I'll give in!
To be furious at falsehood—

              is real goodness!
I'm warning you—

          that fury hasn't left me yet.
And you ought to know—

            I'll stay infuriated for a long time.
There's none of my former shyness left in me.
After all—

       it's more interesting to live

               when you're furious!

How Trifling . . .

How trifling, for the present, in this century,
is the price of human life!
Under Picasso's dove the world
is everywhere at war.

We kiss our wives in a hurry,
give our children a quick hug,
and we leave them, and we fight
in a war of human passions.

We fight with sand and snow,
with the heavens and with the earth.
We fight with lies, with debts,
with idiots and with ourselves.

And when we die, don't dare in your simpleheartedness
to believe it fully,
we don't die of coronaries, or naturally—
we are killed in this war.

And the husbands are blamelessly guilty,
and our wives, leaning from the window,
see them off with the eyes of a soldier's wife,
to this cursed war . . .

Irene

How do you do, Irene
          How are you, Irene?
Without phoning
      I came again,
          for I know
you'll forgive me for this,
you won't send me away again,
but will take me in and give me something to eat,
and will share my sorrows.
I am neither your husband nor your lover,
not even taking off my coat
I hold your hand carefully
          between mine,
and kiss you on the forehead
          while you blush.
You would make such a charming wife—
   devoted,
      loyal,
         responsive.
And my friends would laugh:
        "How could you, Genya!"

Oh think!—
   Who will
      marry her?
How many men has she had in her life—but not one lasted.
Is it possible that she, of all people, could still fall in love?
Because you are
         so kind,
every brute made use of you.
My dearest,
   how
      you were deceived!

How
    you were blemished
             and stained!
And yet your soul—
           is so girlish!
Here you sit,
    shining with goodness,
all shy and childlike.
How could it be
        that now you have
someone to sleep with
          but no one to wake up with?

Once your brown eyes
        were clear,
now your brown eyes are sad,
but they remain beautiful,
pure and kind,
        Russian.
May you meet someone the same,
shining with the same goodness!
May you keep safe not your childish virginity
but the great virginity
        of womanhood.
May you be spared from merciless anguish,
my dearest one,
      tender,
         unfortunate . . .

A Superfluous Miracle

Everything, for heaven's sake, would have been simpler,
and probably kinder and wiser,
if I hadn't rushed to accept a gift
without giving it a thought.

And in the darkness, all my senses aware,
out of those shed clothes was born
this white superfluous miracle
in a dark cloud of sinful hair.

And when I stepped out into the street
I was not expecting what I found—
I heard only snow above me,
I saw only snow beneath me.

The city looked strict, fit for skis,
and the mud hid itself under the snowdrifts,
and the leaning, shrouded cranes
flew motionlessly through the snow.

What for, where from, why?—
by what kind of foolish love
was this new superfluous miracle
suddenly dumped on my shoulders?

Life, it would be better to strike me,
to chop me up for firewood,
than endow me so senselessly—
those gifts are a burden.

You are kind, you can't be faulted,
but there is evil in your tenderheartedness.
If you weren't so beautiful
you wouldn't also be so terrible.

And that god who cries from hidden places
somewhere deep inside me,
is he also (no doubt) a superfluous miracle?
Without him I would be more peaceful . . .

Thus I wandered and wandered along the white deserted
    footpath,
tormenting myself, tormenting someone else,
crushed by the gift of beauty
that mowed me down . . .

White Nights in Archangel

The white nights—the eternal "maybe."
Something is shimmering, strangely worrying me.
Maybe it's the sun, but maybe it's the moon.
Brand new ships' officers wander about,
maybe in Archangel, maybe in Marseille,
maybe in sadness, maybe in joy.

Waitresses, with their eyes rolling
like iceboats beneath their brows,
wander along with them arm in arm.
Can it be the roar of the nor'wester which prompts them
to stop kissing?
Maybe they should, maybe they shouldn't.

The seagulls soar crying over the masts,
maybe they're mourning, maybe they're laughing,
and at the jetty a sailor takes his leave
of a woman, with a long drawn-out kiss:
"What is your name?" "It's not important . . ."
Maybe so, maybe not.

By the jetty the thought comes to me, unbidden,
that the seagulls aren't seagulls, the waves aren't waves,
that he and she—aren't he and she.
All of that is the aurora of the white nights,
all of that is only fancy, fancy,
maybe of insomnia, maybe of a dream.

Now he's going up the gangplank onto his schooner:
"I'll bring you a sealskin!"
But he's forgotten he doesn't know where.
The woman remains standing there in silence.
Who knows—maybe he'll come back.
Maybe no, maybe yes.

The schooner gives a drawn-out hoot of farewell . . .
He doesn't look sad any more.
Now he is sailing, detached and remote,
telling dirty stories with relish
on what may be a sea, on what may be a schooner.
Maybe it's him, maybe somebody else.

And namelessly by the jetty—
maybe it's an end, maybe a beginning—
stands the woman, in a thin gray coat,
slowly melting away like a patch of mist.
Maybe she is Vera, maybe Tamara,
maybe Zoya, but maybe—no one at all . . .

A Ballad about Seals

Papa seal sleeps like a deadbeat.
Mama seal loves her son,
and in her teeth, like sweets,
she carries fish across
to her brown-eyed pup
nicknamed "Little Sprout."

Seals, seals, you are like children—
you should live and go on living,
but long ago you were budgeted for
in the trade estimates,
and mama seals don't know
that radiograms are flying
from Moscow to our schooner.

Somewhere in the city of Boston,
at the fur auction,
a beaming, smart dealer
throws checks around cordially,
exclaiming: "Peace and friendship!
Peace and Russki Little Sprout!"

So that some lady or other,
skinny as a single rib of Adam,
can wrap her joints in furs,
someone with an important expression on his mug
hammers Morse instructions
into our brains.

Seals, seals, we do truly love you,
but we beat you to death with clubs
because our country demands it.
Savagely we bash your eyes in
because you are hard currency,
and we do need hard currency.

Meanwhile the seals are weeping, weeping,
hiding their children under their bellies,
but we can't be sorry for them.
Once more our clubs whistle—
and the screaming eyes of the seals
stick to our huge boots.

And no doubt fish don't want
to be preyed on, but to jump
over the waves, along the waves,
but you seals, you catch them . . .
In nature all things are according to the law.
Fish—for seals. Seals—for us.

All the same, the seals are crying, crying . . .
If only we could change the world—
but it's not our fate to see that!
Seals, we would not have to beat you to death,
we'd drink vodka with you,
we'd play dominoes together.

All things are lawful! Let's double the quota!
All the high-ups are pleased with us!
Why are you sad, like a salmon rolled in batter?
A man with money doesn't get the miseries.
With your pay you can buy
the most perfect of television sets,
let football in the far city of Madrid
fill you with energy.

But suddenly, in a bitter mood
after shouting yourself too many drinks,
when you threaten your wife with the back of your hand,
your nerves without warning give way . . .
you will flinch—her eyes
are screaming at you like those of a seal . . .

The Mail Cutter

The ice had not even begun to break,
no boat could possibly sail yet,
but the letters lay in a pile at the post office,
with all their requests and instructions.

Among them trying vainly to leave,
in the scrawls of the fishermen,
were reproaches, complaints, cries,
awkward confessions of love.

In vain the huskies gazed out to sea,
searching the waves through the fog,
lying like gray hillocks
on the bottoms of overturned boats.

But like a ghost, dreamed up
from the desperate monotony,
the ice-covered mail boat
showed her gray masts.

She was beaten up and dirty,
but to the fishing village
her chilly, husky voice
sounded like the sweetest music.

And the gloomy sailors, throwing us a line
to the shore, like Vikings,
silently, skillfully,
carried canvas sacks full of people's souls.

And again the ship went out, tiredly,
her hull breaking the ice with difficulty,
and I sat in her dank hold
among the piled sacks.

Tormented, I searched for an answer
with all my restless conscience:
"Just what am I, in fact,
and where am I going?

Can it be I am like a frail boat,
and that the passions, like the waves, roll
and toss me about?" But my inner voice
answered me: "You are a mail boat.

Are you tired? Get a grip on yourself . . .
However difficult each foot through the ice,
people are waiting for you.
                              Be courageous.
And be happy.
                    They need you.

Make speed through the angry waves,
heavy with ice,
to all those people who have been separated by the ice,
who are waiting to get in touch again.

And like the first sign of the ship
which people awaited for so long,
carry onward the undying light
of the duty which links us together.

And along the foaming Arctic sea of life,
through all the ice and against the nor'wester,
carry with you those mailbags
full of hopelessness and hopes.

But remember, as you hang on the whistle,
as soon as the storms die down,
steamers, real ships,
will go through these waters, not afraid any more.

And the fishermen, standing up in the barges,
will look admiringly at them,

and their sleek, velvety whistles
will make them forget your husky voice.

But you, with the stink of fish
and blubber oil right through you,
don't lower your rigging gloomily,
You've done the job on schedule.
Be happy then. You are the mail cutter."

Thus the inner voice spoke to me,
impressing upon me the burden of prophecy.
And amid the white night of the Arctic ocean
somehow it was all morning for me.

I didn't think enviously
of someone else, covered with honors,
I was simply happy that a few things
also depended on me.

And covered in someone's fur coat,
I was dependent on so much,
and like that letter of Chekhov's
from little Vanjka Zhukov, simply addressed
"To my grandpa in the village,"
I dozed on heaps of other letters.

Reflections amid the Ice

Self-confidence is a state of grace
but uncertainty is sinful.
It freezes the soul's latent ferment
over, like white ice.

I am superstitiously uncertain.
Hiding my inner qualms,
at times too excessive in some things,
at others constrained and mean.

All the time I repeat to myself:
Why, why do I lie to people,
why do I pretend to be so confident?
when in reality I am not?

The very thought of this stops me
dipping my pen in the ink . . .
O, grant me, God, to be a poet.
And don't let me deceive people.

Why Are You Like This?

When the radio operator of the *Morianna*, head bent,
was searching for a radio beacon,
by chance he picked up on the receiver a woman's voice:
"Why are you like this, why are you like this?"

From Amderma¹ she shouted
across the masts and ice and barking dogs,
and like a storm it grew louder all around:
"Why are you like this, why are you like this?"

Pressing inhumanly against each other,
crunching on all sides against each other,
each ice floe wheezed to the other:
"Why are you like this, why are you like this?"

With all its being the white whale
tangled in the nets cried to the hunter
through a fountain of blood:
"Why are you like this, why are you like this?"

And he, poor fellow,
swept away by a curling wave,
whispered as he perished without trace:
"Why are you like this, why are you like this?"

Like a swine I betray you
and nothing will stop me,
while all the time your eyes implore me:
"Why are you like this, why are you like this?"

You look at me, estranged and full of hate,
already almost like an enemy,
and hopelessly I implore you:
"Why are you like this, why are you like this?"

And heart to heart, nation to nation,
every year more distrustfully
they shout through storms and darkness:
"Why are you like this, why are you like this?"

A Foreigner

> . . . and Mercury floated over us—
> the foreign star.
>
> M. SVETLOV[1]

In Archangel docks there are
foreign vessels,
foreign sorrows,
foreign destinies.

And near the statue of Peter the Great,
Greek sailor, you are weeping till morning,
dark, like a young rook
in the white night.

And in the dusty city square,
it's not foreign at all,
the way you drunkenly wipe your tears
away with a dirty fist.

Maybe the skipper treated you badly?
Maybe someone died in your family?
Maybe you drank too much vodka?
Maybe you are simply not feeling quite yourself?

What experience have you had, Greek,
what has happened to you?
All that has happened to you is
that you too are human.

But there goes the engineer from the Russian schooner,
with gray brows and bronzed face,
half seas over,
suffering from some sort of sorrow.

The engineer sits down by his side.
"Let's have a drink, mate" . . .
And his huge, clumsy hand
reaches silently into his sheepskin coat.

And with skill and concentration
he fishes from his pocket
an interpreter—a little of vodka,
and slaps the seat with a smoked fish.

And they sit and drink in silence,
and embracing each other they stare into the distance,
both of them: Greek sorrow,
and our own Russian grief.

---

[1] Mikhail Arkadjevich Svetlov (1903–1963), a clerk's son, was born in Yekaterinoslav. He took part in the Civil War and during World War II was an army newspaper correspondent. As a poet he is best known for his works on the Revolution and Civil War, such as "Granada" (1926), which develops the theme of international brotherhood and was Mayakovsky's favorite poem.

Jolly Ballad

We had slaughtered a hundred white whales,
civilization was quite forgotten,
our lungs were burned out from smoking shag,
but on sighting port we blew out our chests like barrels
and began to speak to one another politely,
and with the noble air of drinking
we went ashore from the schooner at Amderma.

In Amderma we walked like gods,
swaggering along with our hands on our hips,
and through the port our beards and sidewhiskers
kept their bearings on the pub,
and passing girls and shellbacks
as well as all the local dogs
went along with us as escort.

But, clouding the whole planet,
a notice hung in the shop: "No Spirits!"
We looked at some sparkling wine from the Don
as if it were feeble fruit juice,
and through our agonized yearning
we realized—it wouldn't work.

Now who could have drunk our spirits, our vodka?
It's dreadful the way people drink—simply ruinous.
But skinny as a skeleton, Petka Markovsky from Odessa,
as it always happens with him,
suddenly disappeared somewhere
giving a secretive "Sh–sshh!"

And shortly afterwards, with much clinking,
he turned up with a huge cardboard box,
already slightly merry,

and it was a sweet clinking the box made
as we woke up to the fact: "There she is! She's apples!"
and Markovsky gave us the wink: "She's right!"

We made a splash, waving to everyone—
Chartered a de luxe room in the hotel
and sat down as we were on the bed.
Cords flew off the box
and there, in the glittering columns of the bottles,
bulging, stern, cosy,
absolutely hygienic—
triple-distilled eau de cologne stood before us!

And Markovsky rose, lifting his glass,
pulled down his seaman's jacket,
and began: "I'd like to say something . . ."
"Then say it!" everyone began to shout.
But before anything else
they wanted to wet their whistles.

Markovsky said: "Come on—let's have a swig!
The doctor told me eau de cologne
is the best thing to keep the wrinkles away.
Let them judge us!—we don't give a damn!
We used to drink all sorts of wine!
When we were in Germany
we filled the radiators of our tanks
with wine from the Mosel.

We don't need consumer goods!
We need the wind,
                    the sky!
Old mates, listen to this
in our souls, as though in the safe deposit,
We have the sea, our mothers and young brothers—
All the rest . . . is rubbish!"

Bestriding the earth like a giant,
Markovsky stood with a glass in his hand

that held the foaming seas.
The skipper observed: "Everything is shipshape!"
and only the boatswain sobbed like a child:
"But my mother is dead . . ."

And we all began to burst into tears,
quite easily, quite shamelessly,
as if in the midst of our own families,
mourning with bitter tears
at first for the boatswain's mother,
and afterwards—simply for ourselves.

Already a rueful notice hung in the chemist's shop—
"No Triple Eau de Cologne"—
but eight of us—sea wolves
sobbed over almost all of Russia!—
and in our sobs we reeked
like eight barbershops.

Tears, like tornadoes,
swept away heaps of false values,
of puffed-up names,
and quietly remaining inside us
was only the sea, our mothers and young brothers—
even the mother who was dead . . .

I wept as though I was being set free,
I wept as if I was being born anew,
a different person from what I was,
and before God and before myself,
like the tears of those drunken whalemen,
my soul was pure.

A Ballad about Benkendorf, Chief of Gendarmerie, and Lermontov's Poem "Death of a Poet"

I can imagine the fear and the stupor
when they found, in the office of the secret police,
"Death of a Poet" . . . I can imagine
how all those vile reptiles began to scuttle,
shedding dandruff on their official uniforms,
stuffing their nostrils with purifying snuff.

And the Chief of the Gendarmerie—the leading ideologist,
scalding all subordinate idiots,
put on his glasses . . . On reaching the lines "But there is,
there is Divine Justice, you intimates of corruption . . ."
he shuddered, looked stealthily about him,
and was afraid to read it again.

The cooked-up report was already long ago written,
and Lermontov was packed off to the Caucasus.
But from that moment Benkendorf could no longer sleep.
In the midst of the jests of the court,
in receptions, meetings, ceremonies
"There is Divine Justice . . ." he would hear amid the
    hubbub.
"There is Divine Justice . . ." the blizzard cried in the
    windows.
"There is Divine Justice . . ." the Volga moaned hollowly
through the expanses of the suffering steppes.
"There is Divine Justice . . ." clanked the chains.
"There is Divine Justice . . ." silently cried the eyes
of serfs, taking off their caps.

And the Chief, shaking sweatily with fear,
stealthily turned into an atheist.
The Chief, as always, went to church,
but afterwards in his study he was pleased to reflect

that there isn't a God after all, not in the whole wide
    world,
and that means there is no such thing as Divine Justice.

But for ever—over all the phonies,
gendarmes, suckers-up to the court,
whom their court dress will not save,
the alarm bell resounds inexorably:
"There is Divine Justice, you intimates of corruption . . ."
And the justice of a poet—that is Divine Justice.

To You, People . . .

Along *ulitzas*,
        streets,
                along *rues*
                        and along *calles*
you are walking after work,
                        pushing one another.
I am joining you
                and don't repent of it.
You've become weary
                You've become nervy
You've grubbed down into the bowels of the earth.
                You've reached up to the stars.
But it seems to me—
                You still haven't begun to exist.
In your lips is a Camel,
                a Gitane,
                      a Novostj,
and each of you is like
                      a separate novel,
a separate heart,
                a separate conscience.
Under every beret,
                cap,
                    sombrero,
there is a separate measure for the immeasurable world,
separating beliefs into separate compartments.
But as you drink your absinthe,
                    your vodka,
                        your chianti,
just for a moment you cease to be separate,
and become mankind in your own eyes.
So you can love one another
                    unite your separate novels

into a common novel—
                    your separate consciences
into a common conscience.
I would like to predict all this for you,
and in this prediction not discredit
all that I would like to strengthen
                            in life.

No,
    I am not begging to be a prophet,
                        or a judge,
but you must forgive me—
                    if like a bore I keep on nagging
and repeating to you, the people:
                    "We are people.
                            We are people.

We are people.
            We argue,
                    grumbling and snapping,
at times we jealously trample on one another,
but our separateness—
                    as you know—is false, in general.
We the people
            don't exist separately.
By forgetting others . . .
                    you forget yourself,
by killing others . . .
                    you kill yourself . . ."

Autumn

Inside me the season is autumn,
the chill is in me, you can see through me,
and I am sad, but not altogether cheerless,
and filled with humility and goodness.

But if I rage sometimes,
then I am the one whose rage is shedding my leaves,
and the simple thought comes sadly to me
that raging isn't really what is needed.

The main need is that I should be able
to see myself and the struggling, shocked world
in autumnal nakedness,
when even you, and the world, can be seen right through.

Flashes of insight are the children of silence.
It doesn't matter, if we don't rage aloud.
We must calmly cast off all mere noise
in the name of the new foliage.

Something has apparently happened to me,
and I am relying on nothing but silence,
when the leaves laying themselves one on another
inaudibly become the earth.

And you can see it all, as if from a height,
when you can shed your leaves at the right time,
when without passion inner autumn
lays its airy fingers on your forehead . . .

The Far Cry

A hut is drowsing on the opposite bank.
A horse looms white against the dark meadow.
I call loudly and fire shot after shot
but I cannot wake a soul.

If only the wind would bring them my shots,
if only some dog would hear . . .
They sleep like the dead . . . *The Far Cry*
is the name of the ferry.

My voice has thundered through the halls, like an alarm,
the squares shook to its mighty roll,
but it is too weak to reach
out to this hut, and wake it.

As for the peasants who sleep as though plowing,
breathing heavily, they sleep at their leisure,
they don't hear my voice, any more
than the rustle of the pines and the noise of the rushes.

What sort of an orator are you, what sort of a prophet?
You are confused, soaked and chilled.
Your cartridges are finished. Your voice is getting hoarse.
The rain is flooding your campfire.

But don't grieve that it's vexing enough to make you weep.
You can think deeply, about all sorts of things.
There is plenty of time . . . *The Far Cry*
is the name of the ferry.

The Monologue of the Jukebox

I am an automat
        in the café on the rue Jasmin.
In my glassy womb
        records are on view.
I exist for your joy
        and your horror,
I yell all day long,
        all day long I yell.
Silence is dangerous.
        It's unpatriotic.
I'm on duty
        to keep it away.
Silence
    is pregnant
        with thoughts.
I serve
    as a chucker-out of thoughts.
My owner
        values my work.
I smartly swallow
        centime after centime.
I am aware
        of my clients' demands.
For them, I create
        roaring intimacy.
You want Johnny Holiday?
                    S'il vous plaît!
A drip like Brigitte
                    shivers from weakness.
With plastic tentacles
                    I dig into myself—
and here
    is her Johnny
        screaming under the needle.

Through the door a woman comes in
                    with her pet dog.
A coffee and liqueur?
               S'il vous plaît, madame!
I throw a bridge to your youth
                  across to you.
I put on for you
           an aria by Caruso.
A graying taxi driver
              sits down on a stool,
looks through people
           as if at a mirage.
What are you longing for,
             old Cossack captain?
I'll get "Dark Eyes" for you
             in a flash.
Only sometimes
          playing a Tahitian dance
I anxiously
        consider my own fate.
What kind of a record
           would I put on for myself?
But by now I don't know.
               I'm confused.
Maybe nothing
         would reach me,
maybe nothing
         would please me.
An automat should have no taste.
What they pay me for—
             that's what I'll yell.

And So Piaf Left Us . . .

> *Edith Piaf, the famous French singer, was*
> *known to the public as "the sparrow of Paris."*
> *Teacher of many singers, she was incurably ill*
> *of cancer, but in spite of many operations con-*
> *tinued to sing. A year ago she died, and I had*
> *the chance to be present at her last concert.*

It was a hall in Paris, and in front of the crowd
someone was being extra artistic, jumping around,
dropping witticisms and wriggling about,
and it was all only a prologue—to Piaf.

And then she came on, strangely
resembling a crude small idol,
as if, in a risky little play, tragedy
had wearily blundered in through the wrong door.

Above the nonsense and the clowning
she rose, pale, without strength,
awkward, like a small sparrow with aching eyes,
heavy with her battered wings.

Short, heavily made up,
hiding her cough, barely alive,
she stood astride our time,
her thin legs just holding her up.

She glanced at us, as if at the Seine,
about to step off a cliff down into it,
and I felt like throwing myself at the stage
to hold her up and keep her from falling.

A precise wave of her small wrinkled hand,
and the band began to play . . . she stepped
forward to the edge, aware of her doom,
and, trembling, gathered the music into herself.

And then she sang, taking flight, as if her body,
torn to shreds by surgeons,
was falling from the hold of her eyes
and hoarsely twisting itself into us.

Flying, she sobbed, laughed out loud, whispered,
like the delirious lawns of the Bois de Boulogne,
like a carriage rolling through Saint Germain,
sang a siren's song. That was Piaf.

Alarms and storms and guns merged in her,
pledges, moans and voices of the shadows.
Unwittingly, we had just been kind to her,
like giants to a Lilliputian.

But from her throat rose sorrow, and faith,
and from her throat rose stars, and bells.
And now like a giantess she took us pitiful Lilliputians
playfully in her hands.

The greatest thing of all about her, a true artist,
was that in spite of approaching death,
new artists rose from her throat
leaving lumps of tears in our throats.

Piaf left the stage, prophesying
to us in her exaltation . . .
The little sparrow who sang as the *chimère* of Notre-Dame
would have sung to us, descending to the stage.

Gaston the Eccentric

In Paris lives an eccentric, one Gaston,
a painter and a drunkard.
In summer he loves
          to lie on the lawn,
with his belly
          upwards.

All around him walk the bourgeois
with stones in their kidneys,
holding their fat dogs
on golden chains.

Gaston is too lazy to get up.
He grumbles:
          "Hey, you bums,
we should be creating masterpieces,
masterpieces!"

Gaston picks up a newspaper,
greasy with fingerprints,
but it's all the same stuff in them—
          same as it's been for donkey's years—
some big shot or other
          still talking nonsense.
Gaston sighs:
          "Fancy being dumb enough
to bother about it!

Power is only
          a small blessing,
bad for the nerves.
We should be creating masterpieces,
masterpieces!"

Gaston wanders along
                the rue du Dragon,
his pants hanging down,
and his eyes suffering
for humanity,
                the fools.

Finally, bedraggled,
                covered in dirt
from Cadillacs,
Gaston knocks on the shutters
of remittance men
                and dealers.

"Enough of puffing out your chests
and gulping sherbets!
We should be creating masterpieces,
masterpieces!"

Know this—
                at least—
                        Gaston
won't be humble,
there's only one of him,
                but he's with Rimbaud,
he's with Verlaine.

And Rembrandt's Saskia
Sitting on his knees
laughs down the centuries,
all powerful over your deformities,
                        you cripples!

Why summon parliament
or carry out maneuvers?
We should be creating masterpieces,
masterpieces!

Colosseum

Colosseum,
    I have not come to you, as to a museum.
I am not one of your traipsing tourists.
Our meeting—
        is the meeting of two old friends
and old enemies,
            Colosseum.
You hoped in vain for my death.
I have come back,
            forgotten by you,
as to the place
            where I had killed a thousand times
and where, a thousand times, I myself had been killed.
Your lions
        stroked me with their paws—
a terrible caress.
To the gladiator—
        the lot of the gladiator,
Colosseum,
    for ever and ever.
Languidly,
    arrogantly,
you wanted me, for no cause at all,
to die a beautiful death
            in the arena,
but no one dies beautifully.
And when,
        no longer feeling the spears,
I fell down,
    dying like an animal,
I saw
    a down-pointed thumb
even in
    a raised one . . .
I have come back like vengeance—
    no vengeance could be more terrible.

Did you not expect it, Colosseum?
>   Tremble, Colosseum!
I have come not in daytime
>   but at the dead of night,
when all your guides—
>   your spivs are dead to the world,
and all around—
>   only the stink of dogs' piss,
empty cans,
>   broken bricks . . .
In spite of the loudest yells
>   and deepest roars—
in my body
>   swords twist,
splinters of claws,
>   and the slivers of passions . . .
Once more I can hear
>   the crunch of sweets in the teeth
>   of children in the stands,
accompanying the crunch of Christian bones.
Colosseum,
>   have you got out of the habit of such amusements?
What's on the program tonight, Colosseum?
Fearless rats scour about
in the kingdom of night and ruins.
Powdered pederasts
hug one another near the lion's gate.
In the box once used by Nero
a society lady shudders with delight.
There's a rustle of nylon—
a gigolo pulling off her pants.
There, where it smells of murder,
where the white bones of my dear ones lie buried,
a prostitute briskly
squats down for a quick piss.
There, where we gladiators
>   perished miserably,
someone peers into people's faces:
"Heroin . . . Anybody want some heroin?"
Colosseum,

accept
>   this vengeance
without complaint,
>   and don't blame fate.
That which is built on blood,
itself shall bleed to death.
But I am telling you,
>   Colosseum,
>   without any irony:
at times I grow cold with terror.
Only on the surface is Nero missing
from this world—
>   which is the Colosseum all over again.
True, they are splitting atoms,
climbing out into cosmic space,
but even now the world is divided
into spectators
>   and gladiators.
I don't want to offend the gladiators:
with all my skin and my guts I feel sorry for them,
but I hate the spectators:
Nero is still alive in every one of them.
Yes, those sated spectators
>   are terrifying,
shouting from their seats:
>   "Hit him!
>   Kill him!"
But the most terrifying spectators of all—
are those who make a profit from blood.
You promoters
>   and cheerleaders,
you urge them on shamelessly.
Do you want
>   us gladiators
always to be killing one another?
You howling furies
>   and urgers,
screaming from your safe seats
that we
>   should not be cowards

that we
>   should push against the sword, beautifully . . .
I curse you,
>   with your Nero-like gestures,
but listen,
>   you scoundrels:
in the world there are
>   executioners and victims,
but there is also a third lot:
>   fighters!
Longing for comradeship
>   I wander,
stumbling, I wander through the ages,
and in my gladiator's dreams
I see a new Spartacus.
Now I stand in the center of the arena
in front of the auditorium, which is seething like hell.
I'm weary,
>   exhausted,
>   covered with wounds,
but I do not fall:
>   they won't have mercy on me.
In the noise
>   I can hear the roar of the waiting lion.
The whole theater is torn to pieces beneath his claws.
They hurl questions at me
>   like darts,
but my skin—
>   is my only shield.
Colosseum,
>   applaud,
>   gape at me!
Curse you,
>   Colosseum, executioner!
And thank you for the lesson!
Through the shouting and screaming
I raise over you
>   my avenging hand
and mercilessly—
>   point my thumb down . . .